W9-BRR-825

THE
RIPKEN
WAY

THE
RIPKEN
WAY

A MANUAL FOR BASEBALL AND LIFE

CAL RIPKEN, SR.
WITH LARRY BURKE
FOREWORD BY CAL RIPKEN, JR.

POCKET BOOKS
NEW YORK LONDON TORONTO SYDNEY TOKYO SINGAPORE

POCKET BOOKS, a division of Simon & Schuster Inc.
1230 Avenue of the Americas, New York, NY 10020

ISBN: 0-671-02775-1

First Pocket Books hardcover printing May 1999

10   9   8   7   6   5   4   3   2   1

POCKET and colophon are registered trademarks of
Simon & Schuster Inc.

Designed by Joseph Rutt

Printed in the U.S.A.

To my wife, Vi; daughter, Ellen; and sons,
Cal, Jr.; Fred; and Bill.
The closeness of family while traveling all over the
country made the game of life and the game of
baseball so great.

—C.R.

With love to Beth, Casey, Maddie, and Charlie.

—L.B.

CONTENTS

FOREWORD

. . . Let me start by thanking my dad. He inspired me with his commitment to the Oriole tradition and made me understand the importance of it. He not only taught me the fundamentals of baseball, but he also taught me to play it the right way, and to play it the Oriole way. From the very beginning, my dad let me know how important it was to be there for your team and to be counted on by your teammates.

Those are my words, from the speech I made on September 6, 1995, at Baltimore's Camden Yards, after I had broken Lou Gehrig's record by playing in my 2,131st consecutive game. I paid tribute to a number of people that night, but I started with my dad because, well, that's where the Streak, which ended in 1998 at 2,632 games, really started.

Would there have been a streak had it not been for the lessons of discipline, dedication, determination, and desire that my father taught me? Heck, there might not have been a *career* were it not for my dad. There might not even have been a big-league appearance.

I probably had the talent, genetically speaking, to be a pretty good baseball player. I most likely would've had enough ability to get drafted, but beyond that I could very well have been a statistic, like most minor leaguers—about three percent of whom actually make it to the majors. Without Dad's influence I might not have made it all. I almost surely wouldn't have had the career that I've had. I certainly wouldn't have had the desire to be in the lineup every day, or understand the importance of that.

Dad impressed upon me from the beginning that in order to do anything well, you have to work at it. And in order to work at something you have to really love it and understand the value and the product of your work. Obviously, in baseball, you have to have the talent first, but once you have the talent the thing that makes you better—in baseball or in anything you do—is hard work. That lesson was the biggest and best gift that my dad gave me. He also gave me his passion for the sport, the great feeling of wearing the uniform, his love of the game, his willingness to work at everything he did, and his satisfaction in the rewards of that work. I came to understand and appreciate all of those things at a very early age.

You can't truly understand it all unless you're willing to work. You have to be willing to lay it on the line first. But once you do, there's a very complete and satisfying feeling, and nobody can take that away from you. Without my father's influence, though, without that real strong guidance, I probably would've washed out of baseball eventually. The funny thing is, as valuable as these lessons were, I don't think Dad even knew he was giving them to me, because he wasn't teaching me directly, he was simply showing it all to me by being himself.

My dad has always been a great teacher of the game of baseball. He does that with words and demonstrations, almost like a teacher in a classroom would. But many of the big things I learned from him—in baseball and in life—I learned just by watching him. For instance, you can speak of a work ethic, but how do you really teach that? The only way you get it across is by showing it, by living it.

And that's how my father has lived his life, how he has gone about doing things: his routines, the way he dives in, organizes and just attacks any kind of work, his ability to identify the things that need to be done and do them. He's a real hands-on doer in all facets of his life.

I've always been willing to work hard to get better in baseball, and I'm willing to do that in most areas of my life. My dad is the same way—that's his personality, that's what he does. And I really picked up on that.

When the Orioles moved to a new spring training site, they needed to decide how to set up the ball fields, where the dormitory was going to go, and so forth. Dad always took on the problems and became the foreman of the job, but he was also out there doing the work, too. He'd actually be digging out fields, measuring the bases, cutting the diamond, leveling the infield, putting down the grass seed, pouring the concrete for the dugouts, and putting the backstops up.

That's so typical of him. When the Orioles moved their spring training camp from Fernandina Beach, north of Jacksonville, to Biscayne College (which is now St. Thomas University) in the Miami suburb of Opa-Locka, Dad supervised the construction crew—and did a lot of the work himself. This was all while spring training was going on, and he was running the camp at the same time! He'd be a baseball guy during the day—starting with his morning meetings and all the way through to the game or whatever activities ended the day—and then he'd go to work on the construction job. He wouldn't even take his uniform off, he'd just take a little time to eat a bit of a sandwich or something and then jump on the tractor. Sometimes he'd work so long that he had to turn on the tractor's headlights.

People can talk about work ethic, but the more they talk about it, the less they do. My dad's not a talker, he's a doer. So I just watched him, and that's how I found out how to do the right thing. I learned that if I wanted something done the right way, and I wanted it done to my own high standards, only I could do it. And I think that's a great, great trait.

He passed on his love of baseball to me in the same way: by example. As a kid I had a chance to witness it by going to the ballpark with him and being in his environment. Sometimes, at home, it could seem a little like a business. He had a lot of administrative responsibilities, such as typing out paperwork for the organization.

He was required to file daily reports on each player, in triplicate, and include the box score from the local newspaper. I still remember Old One-Finger, as Mom called him, pecking away on that Smith-Corona. He didn't have as much time to play with us as he would've liked, but we could see his joy for sports when we had the opportunity.

When I had a chance to ride in the car with him to the ballpark, I could see his whole world open up. I wouldn't call it a personality change, but once Dad put that uniform on, there was this comfort, this joy, this passion for who he was and what he was doing that was just a great thing to see. He used to say, "There's something to putting this uniform on. These are my work clothes." And he really meant it.

The first thing he did when he got to the ballpark was put that uniform on, and he did it very quickly. When he walked through the door there was no BS'ing, there was no walking around being sociable. He put the uniform on, then the day started. The last thing he did before he went home was take it off. But at the end of the day it was difficult to get that uniform off his body— he didn't want to take it off.

That's the kind of love for baseball that I took from being around my father. I discovered it for myself, by being around him, and then I started to feel the same thing. He never preached it, I just watched him and I saw it. It was almost like he had a secret that the rest of us didn't know, and I was curious to find out what that secret was.

Once I was old enough, I was around the ballpark all day for much of the summer. I had to wear a uniform, too—no shagging balls in shorts, that was one of my dad's real pet peeves. He told me, "If you're out there on the field, look like you belong." There were so many advantages to being around professional players. I could ask advice on every position. I'd gather information from a variety of sources, but I'd always test it against Dad's knowledge, to find out if I was searching out the right people to tell me things.

Once my father got into his pregame routine, I had very little one-on-one time with him. I know he loved me being there, but he had to focus on his job, so I talked to a lot of the players. There were always a few moments at the end of the day where Dad and I could catch up, though. He'd be going over his pitching charts and various other things, and I'd be sitting there watching him. I can still remember sitting on the floor, leaning against the wall, just taking it all in, and thinking that it was almost time for us to leave. I'd be looking forward to those few minutes when he and I could just talk.

Finally Dad would look over and ask me, "What'd you do today? Is there anything you picked up?" I might say, "I talked to Doug DeCinces about fielding ground balls today, and he showed me this and that." I was always looking for my father's approval on what I had learned. I'd ask, "Is that right?" And he'd say, "You know, that's exactly right. He's very fundamentally sound." So then I knew that the guy who had given me the tip was someone who I wanted to hang out with, because my dad had said he had good baseball advice. But if I had, say, an outfielder who was messing around with me, telling me, "Catch the ball with one hand over here like this," or, "It's better to do it this way," it was a different story. I had a feeling when I got certain information that it wasn't correct, but I'd tell Dad anyway. And he'd say, "No, that's not right. Who said that to you?" Then I'd cross that guy off my list. I wouldn't seek him out for information anymore. That was my system.

My goal when I was a kid was always to get time with my father by myself. When he was managing in the minor leagues, Dad frequently ran promotional clinics for the club on Saturday mornings. The idea was to bring the community and the baseball team together by teaching the sport. My sister and brothers and I started out going to these clinics with my dad, but we soon realized how boring they were. Elly, Fred, and Bill would say, "It's kind of fun to go there, but sitting there in the hot sun in the bleachers, just listening to Dad talk over and over again about the same thing, that's not fun. I'd rather stay home and do something else." I, on the other hand, recognized an opening.

So when my dad would come in our bedrooms on Saturday morning and tap each of us on the leg and say, "You want to go with me to the clinic?" you'd hear, "No." "No." "No." But I'd say, "Yeah, sure," even though I felt the same way as my sister and two brothers. I didn't want to go, either, but I realized that I'd be in the car by myself with Dad for however long the ride was to and from the clinic. The middle part—sitting through the clinic—was a sacrifice, but in the end it was a very valuable sacrifice, because while he was teaching everybody else he was teaching me at the same time. I remember those moments from my childhood—the end of the day in the manager's office, the car rides—as the most important times.

When I was growing up, my father couldn't be around enough to be my day-to-day coach. Mom was always there to take me to events, because Dad had baseball obligations. But once I started to advance to the higher levels of the game, high school and beyond, I began to relate some of my baseball difficulties to my dad. I could tell him something was wrong, and even over the phone he could almost always say something that would correct the problem. He'd ask, "Where are you hitting the ball? What happens when you swing? What do you feel?" He'd provide a diagnosis, like a doctor, without even seeing me. Based on all his experience he'd be able to offer a solution.

It always amazed me. I'd say, "I'm popping the ball to third," or, "I'm popping the ball up to first," and he'd say, "You need to wait a little longer," or, "It sounds to me like you're staring at the pitcher instead of just letting your eyes relax. Look at the second baseman and then take your eyes back to the pitcher," or, "Concentrate on taking the bat back just a little bit and keeping your front shoulder in." Those little things always seemed to fix the problem.

Then when I got to the big leagues and Dad was there to see things with his own eyes as well as be my instructor, he was able to detect problems before I actually got to the point of frustration and had to ask him. Now, he sees the games on TV, so I'll call him up and we'll talk, and he'll sometimes throw out some things. I'm not as reliant on him as I used to be, mostly because he has put all that information, all the little fixes, in my head.

My father has always had the discipline and determination necessary to solve any problem. At family gatherings we'll sometimes bring up this story: Dad takes great pride in his garden, and was furious when he returned home from a road trip one summer to find that a groundhog had eaten his prized crop of watermelons and cantaloupes. The next morning at dawn he took his thermos of coffee, pack of cigarettes, and newspaper and sat by the garden with a shotgun. Some say he did this for three or four straight days, but I think that's an exaggeration. It was at least one or two, though. Anyway, Dad was there, waiting, when the groundhog came out and headed for the string beans. From the house, just one shotgun blast was heard. It was a task that had to be done—that's basically the story. My dad has a streak in him, an old farmer's streak, of persistence and stubbornness. Some people think those qualities are negative, but I think they're positive.

Those traits definitely showed in my father's physical durability. He has a way of telling stories that minimize the effect of his injuries. I think the biggest impact he had on me, in terms of how I deal with what people sometimes call nagging injuries, is that there was a certain honor in his stories. I gained a great deal of respect for the strength he showed and the way he played through pain.

He once told me about the game he caught in the Susquehanna League, in which a foul tip went off his hand and pushed back the skin so that the bone was sticking out of his finger. The manager supposedly came out and said, "You're coming out of the game," and my dad said, "The hell I am. I'm catching this game, we're winning, and I'm going to see it through." He'd tell stories in which he actually got into arguments like that with his manager. He'd say something like, "Just tape this up. Am I going to hurt it any more than it already is? Can this wait an hour or two hours?" and the manager would say, "Okay." Dad had the ability to get his way in that regard. Earl Weaver, or whoever the manager was, might say, "You throw a ball away and I'm taking your butt out of here." But my father would respond, "You just get back there, I'll take care of things out here, you take care of over there."

He told me he had a softball mask on one time, and the mask had a wide space between the bars that you could see through. A softball couldn't fit through there, but the head of a bat could. One time a hitter apparently followed through on his swing and the bat came flying through those bars and banged Dad right in the nose.

He'd get spiked, and with his Rambo-type attitude take a needle and thread and sew it up himself. That didn't actually happen, but those were the kind of stories he'd tell. It was sort of expected of me—this is the way it is. I wanted to make my dad proud, so when I had an injury, I said, "That's okay, I'll get through it." That became my mentality.

When he took us kids out and hit ground balls to us, he'd say, "The ball only weighs five-and-a-quarter ounces. How much can it hurt?" He knew the ball *could* hurt us, and we felt the ball hitting us, but we didn't want him to know that it had hurt us. If we got hit by a ball, he'd first look to see how badly we were hurt, then if it wasn't serious he'd say, "It's just a bruise. Put a little tobacco juice on it and it'll be all right." Or he'd say, "It'll be all right before you're married twice." He didn't believe in babying us, but he'd be the first to determine how severe an injury was. He'd act like a trainer when he had to, but if we were okay then it was "Come on, let's go again."

That brings to mind another famous story in Ripken family lore: Our neighborhood in Aberdeen was small, and the snowplows didn't get to it that often. Every once in a while when it would snow hard, my dad would plow the neighborhood. There was this tractor in the barn that belonged to a guy for whom my father used to do some work. Dad had a key for this old tractor, so when it snowed he'd sometimes go up there, start it up, and use this box drag that he had built—a triangular wooden drag that he'd pull behind the tractor and use to plow the roads. He took great satisfaction in being able to do that for our little neighborhood.

One winter day we went up there to use the tractor, but the battery was dead. You could crank this old tractor by hand, so Dad picked the crank up, this big metal rod, and let us feel how heavy it was. Then he said, "Okay, I'm going to show you how to crank a tractor." Fred and I looked at each other as if to say, "When are we ever going to crank a tractor?" But that's the way my father is—he wanted to teach us while he was doing this task.

So he started to crank it, and he explained, "You let the torque of the engine bring the crank back up and then you push it down again. Never windmill it." But the tractor wasn't starting up. Dad looked at it and said, "I'm going to do this, but I never, ever want to see you do it." So he started cranking the thing windmill-style— like he had just told us never to do—pushing it down and pulling it up. I'm not sure if it backfired or what, but the crank came flying off, and this big old metal rod hit Dad in the middle of the forehead. A cut immediately opened up, and he got this big, bright-eyed look on his face like he didn't know where he was. Then the blood started spewing out, and I started to panic. I had just gotten my driver's license, so immediately I was thinking we should put him in the car and drive him to the emergency room.

Dad took an oily rag out of his pocket and stuck it up on his forehead for a minute. He was starting to get his senses back, like a boxer who'd taken a shot to the head.

Then he said, "Okay, let's go." I assumed he knew the seriousness of the injury. It was about a ten-minute drive to the hospital, but we had to go by our house on the way. I was driving and my dad didn't say a word, he was just holding that oily rag on his head. But as we got close to the house he said, "Just pull in here for a minute."

I figured we were going to stop by our house, pick up Mom, and head over to the hospital. Well, we pulled up and Dad got out of the car, didn't say a word, walked into the house, didn't tell Mom anything, walked straight into the bathroom, and shut the door. I ran in yelling, "Mom! Mom! Dad cut his head!" And she was running around saying, "Where is he?" We couldn't find him.

He had locked the bathroom door and wouldn't let us in. In there, he took these butterfly bandages and doctored himself up, putting four or five of them on so that they pretty much closed up the wound. Then he put a bigger Band-Aid over it, and he got back in the car with Fred and me.

Now I still thought we were going to the hospital. We started to drive out and I was about to turn right, toward the hospital, but instead Dad said, "Left." We went back up to the barn, he cranked the tractor up, and plowed the neighborhood. He never went to the doctor. It was a pretty big gash—he should have gotten stitches. He had a big scar at the time, but he healed up pretty well.

After witnessing that incident, I have to think that it probably is true that the bat came through the catcher's mask and hit him in the nose. It probably is true that this bone was sticking out of his hand and he didn't think it was necessary to go to the hospital. But my dad doesn't brag about those things. That's just who he is. That's what he gave to me as far as being tough.

You don't set out to do something like the Streak. It certainly wasn't a goal of mine. Dad taught me how to play the game, and there's a certain expectation from that approach, what your responsibilities are. Executing that approach means coming to the ballpark and saying to your manager, I'm ready to play for you. And if you want to put me in there, it's my job to give you everything I have.

The Streak was born because my father taught me to come to the ballpark with a desire and a passion to play, and the manager actually wrote my name in the lineup every day. One thing I always thought was funny was that as the Streak went on, people said that nobody could stop it, that I had power over everybody else. Every manager who came in couldn't take me out of the lineup, even if they had wanted to. When I hear that kind of thing I just laugh. I've always said, Wait a minute, you're making these assumptions, but what did I do as a twenty-one-year-old? Did I call Earl Weaver into *my* office and say, "Listen, Earl, I'm playing in every single game. You're just going to do it and worry about everybody else later." That's ridiculous. The reason the Streak continued is that the managers kept writing my name on the lineup card, and I kept doing what I was supposed to do, the way my dad had taught me. It was very simple.

I wanted to make Dad proud of me. I wanted to do what I thought was right. Even if I felt like I was injured, it became a mind-over-matter situation. I wanted to prove that I was like him. If I got hit with a pitch on the hand or on the elbow, or turned an ankle, and people said, "You probably should sit down for a few days or that's going to blow up," I'd say, "Let's see how it feels. Tape it up a little tighter and I'll see if I can do it." It was the same way I had seen my father do it.

Dad has always said that baseball is a lot like life, and he's right. I've always found myself relating his baseball lessons to life lessons, and that's what this book is all about. But if you're going to really help somebody, and be a leader, first you have to have the respect and credibility to actually teach and lead. My father has always had those.

I watched Dad for years, how he maintained his respect for people, the dignity he displayed in his teaching. All of that has helped me with my baseball skills, and it has also helped me with my people skills. I've built up a lot of credibility in the game by being consistent with these philosophies. There's a lot of substance to them, and you can apply them in all areas of life: Work hard. Communicate. Use your head. Don't pretend to be someone you're not. And those are the things I've always tried to do.

—Cal Ripken, Jr.

INTRODUCTION

It wouldn't be much of a stretch to say that baseball
is my life. I spent thirty-eight years—more than 60 percent of my entire life—as a player, coach, manager, and
scout in the professional ranks with the Baltimore
Orioles, and I remain active in the game today through
my involvement with the Cal Ripken Baseball School in
Emmitsburg, Maryland.

I broke in with the Orioles organization in 1957, as
a catcher with the Class C Phoenix Stars, and soon
thereafter I began keeping notes on the things we did—
baseball technique, strategy, drills, and the rest. I continued adding to my notes as my playing days wound
down and my minor-league managerial career began in
the early 1960s. The manager of the Orioles at that time,
Paul Richards, had a very small baseball manual that he
sent to his minor-league managers, because he wanted
his people in the farm system to know how certain
things should be done.

As I moved up the ladder in the Orioles system,
from Class D Leesburg, Florida, to Triple A Rochester,
New York, and ultimately to Baltimore, I kept adding to

my notes. I would often scribble in the margins of the Paul Richards manual, some of which had become out-dated over the years. Finally, in 1986, I decided to write my own manual: the way I thought baseball should be played. Well, I had written so many things into the Paul Richards manual by that point that I had to do quite a bit of deciphering in places where I had crossed out and hen-scratched in underneath. I wanted my manual to go into much greater detail: From having played, coached, and watched the game for more than thirty years, these were the things that I thought had to be done by an indi-vidual, or by a team, to be successful.

Although I was pleased with the finished product, I decided not to have my manual published at that time. It served primarily as the curriculum at my baseball school. But over the past thirteen years many people who have seen *The Cal Ripken Baseball Manual for Players* have been impressed not only by its sound instructional content but also by its broader wisdom. Several people have told me that because my manual stresses the importance of playing smart and practic-ing correctly, and also contains some other valuable life lessons, it would be of great use to players and coaches in other sports, and maybe even to non-athletes.

Do I think I have all the answers? Not even close. But I do believe that I have a wealth of experience in the game of baseball, and I also believe that baseball is really just a walk of life. So I felt that at the very least I had some useful advice to pass along. But rather than simply publishing my manual, which contains a great

deal of technical information and could well be intimi-
dating to all but the serious player, I decided to write
a book that delivered the instructional component
and real-life wisdom of my manual in an easier-to-read
format. And so *The Ripken Way* was born.

PROLOGUE

A few months back I got a call from a young guy who had played ball for me years ago in the Baltimore Orioles' minor-league system. He had been released after about three years in our organization. He had some ability, but he just wasn't blessed with enough to continue on through the minor leagues. There was always going to be somebody coming along who was better than he was. But he got to Class C ball before he was released; at the time there was Class D, C, B, A, Double A, Triple A, and then the major leagues.

He's now in business for himself, in a completely different field. And in the process of our conversation, he told me, "The things that you taught me in baseball—the things that *you* as an individual stressed to me—I still apply every day." Well, that gives me a lot of satisfaction, there's no question. And, sure, I tend to glow a little bit, because now I know that I accomplished something for the good, and it came out all right.

That's why I always tell my players, when you talk about baseball and life, they're the same thing. Baseball's just a walk of life. Everything you do in this game you do in life, and everything you do in life you do in this game.

And that's the idea of this book: that by talking about the game of baseball—my life in the game, which is where we'll start off; playing the game; Cal Jr.'s career; managing and coaching; some topics outside the lines; and my family—we're really talking about the game of life. The same lessons that help you on the ball field will help you off of it, too.

I'm not out to give a lot of technical instruction here, although I definitely think that the concepts covered in these pages will help make you a better ballplayer. By covering those areas of the game that have the broadest applications to life, though, such as the value of discipline, hard work, and communication, and the importance of using your head, mastering the fundamentals, and being able to adjust, I hope to help you become a better employee, a better boss, a better student, a better teacher—a better person—whatever your walk of life.

CHAPTER 1

MY LIFE
IN BASEBALL

A Chance to Play

People talk about the game of baseball being very tough to play, especially at the major-league level. But when I was playing professionally, in the late 1950s and early '60s, I didn't look at it that way. I always enjoyed playing the game, and at the professional level I had the opportunity to play it—a lot. I was tickled to death with that. In the pros you get the opportunity to play every day, so I really didn't look at anything as being tough.

THE EARLY DAYS

My father, Arend Ripken, was killed in a car crash when I was nine. He really didn't play that much baseball, but he was always interested in the game. I got involved in baseball because of my two older brothers, Oliver—eighteen years older than I, and Bill—ten years older—who played baseball and softball. We were a baseball family.

I just loved the game from a very young age. I've always said that I was a better hitter at four than I was at twenty-four, because as a little kid I was always out in the yard with a ball, a bat, and a glove.

As a boy I was more of a player than a fan, because we were out in the country, and the only way we could follow major-league baseball games was on the radio. We had a Triple A club in Baltimore at the time, but no major-league team until 1954.

My brothers and I played together for the Aberdeen Canners in a Sunday-afternoon league called the Susquehanna League. Ours was an amateur team, although it was kind of a semi-pro league.

Ollie, who like our father worked for a retail lumber company, was the catcher and Bill played centerfield.

When I moved up from batboy to catch for the team, Ollie moved to rightfield. Ollie was a good hitter who won the league's batting title, and a good defensive player, well-rounded in all facets of the game, who could've had the opportunity to play professional ball had World War II not entered the picture.

Bill was a great outfielder with an excellent arm, and he was a good hitter, too. He could run, he could throw, he could field, and he could hit. He was a very good two-strike hitter. But at that time there were a lot more farm clubs than there were major-league clubs.

Bill was signed by the Brooklyn Dodgers, and he made it to Triple A, with the Montreal Royals of the International League. After four years he quit pro ball and took a job in a bank. Branch Rickey even tried to talk him out of it, but Bill was tired of all the traveling and just felt that he didn't want to do it anymore. It's just my opinion, but I think if he would've stayed one more year he would've gone on to the big leagues.

I was a better hitter at four than I was at twenty-four, because as a little kid I was always out in the yard with a ball, a bat, and a glove.

DOING IT ALL

In the minor leagues I did it all: I managed, I played—I even drove the bus. I did all three in 1962 at Appleton, Wisconsin. I always said I got the managing job in Appleton because I had driven the bus for half a year in 1960, after Earl Weaver, who was the manager in Appleton at the time, fired the bus driver. Everyone said, "Ripken will drive the bus," and so I wound up driving it the rest of the year. Then when I went back to Appleton to manage in '62, Ollie Lindquist, who owned the bus company, wouldn't give the ball club the bus unless I drove it.

I enjoyed every day I spent in the minor leagues. I enjoyed every day I spent in the big leagues. I would go back and do everything exactly the same as I did the first time. There's only one thing I probably wouldn't do.

In 1957, when I was playing in Phoenix, the clutch on the bus was slipping as we were halfway up a mountain. The bus driver got the bus off to the side of the road, and I said I'd adjust the clutch, because I had a little bit of a mechanical background with vehicles. I told the bus driver to turn the wheels of the bus all the way to the left, and I got under the bus and adjusted the clutch. Then we drove on over the mountain successfully and got to our destination.

Well, as I said, there's one thing I'd change: If I had that to do again, I'd tell the bus driver to let the wheels of the bus stay straight. With those wheels turned, if the brakes had failed and the bus had drifted backward, it would've run right over me.

In the minor leagues I did it all: I managed, I played—I even drove the bus.

FROM PLAYER TO MANAGER

Sometimes you'll hear people talk about a particular player in terms of what kind of a coach or manager he would make. But I can tell you that as a player, I wasn't thinking about that sort of thing—I was just concentrating on playing the game and moving up the ladder. I guess when I was in the minor leagues I probably thought in the back of my mind that if I was unable to move up as a player, or if something happened as far as an injury, I would want to stay in the game as a manager or a coach. But you don't give much thought to that when you're playing.

Here's how I first came to consider managing: It was in March of 1961, and I was twenty-five years old, coming off my best year in the minor leagues—a .281 average and 74 RBIs in 107 games at Class B with the Orioles' Fox Cities affiliate in Appleton, Wisconsin, while playing for a twenty-nine-year-old manager by the name of Earl Weaver. (Cal Jr. was born on August 24, 1960, so that had been a pretty good year all around.) I was catching for Rochester, Baltimore's Triple A club, in a spring training game in Daytona, and I got hit on the right shoulder with two foul balls in succession. I didn't think too much of it at the time, because after that happened I still threw two guys out at second base.

But the next day when I came to the park, I couldn't hold on to the ball. I went to play catch on the side and the ball fell right out of my hand. I went to Jim Dudley, our trainer, and said, "Dud, I can't throw the ball." He thought I was kidding, because I kidded around a lot with him, but then he realized that I was serious. There wasn't a lot he could do, though. When I finally was able to get a hold of the ball and throw it, my shoulder hurt terribly. I couldn't throw, which meant I lost strength in the shoulder. They sent me to the Orioles' Double A club in Little Rock, Arkansas, where the climate was a lot warmer, which they thought might help, and I played in thirty-two games there, but the shoulder just got progressively worse.

That's when I began thinking about trying a year managing in the minor leagues. As it so happened, Harry Dalton, the Orioles farm director, called me and said, "I've got a managing job for you." All I said was, "Thank you." I didn't ask where, when, how much money, or anything else. I went to Class D Leesburg, Florida, to manage, as a replacement for Billy DeMars, who had just been promoted to Class B. I managed my first game with Leesburg on June 7, 1961, and I wound up playing fifty-two games there as well.

I was young for a manager—because a guy of twenty-five was usually still playing, or if he didn't have a lot of talent he was released and was out of baseball—but by that point in my playing career I had shown the ability to run a ball club. I was a catcher, and the catcher ran the ball game. I moved people around on the field and showed that I knew the game and could handle people.

The kids in Class D were seventeen, eighteen, nineteen years old, and in those days when you were managing you weren't just the manager, you were the pitching coach, you were the hitting coach, you were every kind of coach. I didn't have a coach working with me in the minor leagues until Chico Fernandez coached for me at Rochester in 1969.

As a player, I had shown the ability to run a ball club. I was a catcher, and the catcher ran the ball game. I moved people around on the field and showed that I knew the game and could handle people.

In mid-August, after about ten weeks with Leesburg, I went back to Rochester because they needed a catcher, and I finished the season playing in eleven games there. The next year I continued to manage and play in the minor leagues, this time with the Class D club in Appleton, but I knew by the end of that season that I wasn't going to play any more because of my shoulder. Had it not been for the injury I probably would've played at least a few more years, but a catcher who can't throw does more harm than good.

They found out that those foul balls back in March of '61 had knocked the deltoid muscle back and out of place, and the whole shoulder had been set incorrectly for a three- or four-month period. We were able to work on it and get it back in place, but the muscle that I used to throw with—that comes up my arm and goes to my shoulder and down my back—had shrunk. It was a matter of being able to get that muscle stretched out to where it should be, and that took a long, long time. In fact, it was six years before I threw without pain.

I was probably the one who started the practice of managers and coaches throwing batting practice from in front of the pitching rubber, because I threw batting practice every day in Leesburg from about forty-five feet away. The groundskeepers would get mad at me because I was stepping on the edge of their grass in front of the mound. Once I got the muscle stretched out, and I was able to throw without pain, I continued to throw batting practice every place I ever coached or managed. In the big leagues, there was many a time that I'd throw for an hour and a half of early hitting, and then throw to my regular group for fifteen or twenty minutes of regular hitting.

My injury was just one of those freak accidents that happens. Fortunately for me I was able to come up with a managing job and stay in baseball, move along, and eventually get to the big leagues as a coach and manager.

BROTHER JIMMY

I don't know if there's anyone in the game of baseball with whom I have more of a history, or to whom I'm closer, than Jimmy Williams. He's almost like a brother to me, considering that his association with my family dates back to 1947.

Jimmy and my brother Bill both signed with the Dodgers in '47, and they played the outfield together and roomed together at Danville in '48. I played against Jimmy when we were both in the Texas League in the late '50s. In the early '60s, when he was managing in the Dodger organization and, of course, I was managing in the Oriole organization, Jimmy was at Grand Forks in the Northern League when I was at Aberdeen, South Dakota. In the early '70s, he was at Columbus, Georgia, in the Houston organization, when I was at Asheville, North Carolina, in the Southern League.

After that he came over to our organization, managed Cal at Double A Charlotte in 1980, and came to the big leagues as a coach in 1981. He and I were both coaches on the Oriole club from '81 to '86, and he was my third base coach in '87, when both Cal and Bill were on the club. And he would've been my third base coach in '88 too, if Mr. Edward Bennett Williams, the owner, hadn't been so insistent on making a change.

Jimmy is like part of the family. We're still close— Jimmy lives in Joppa, which is just fifteen miles down the road, and he and his wife and Vi and I play a lot of golf together.

Jimmy was a very good teacher and a very good instructor, and he was a good manager and a good coach. He was just a good baseball man. He was brought up in the Dodger organization, which is a very fundamentally sound organization, and he was as responsible as anyone for making the Orioles a solid organization.

He was a very well-rounded baseball man. He managed in the minor leagues at the time when you didn't have coaches, so he was the manager, the pitching coach, the hitting coach, the infield coach, and the outfield coach. I went through that same training process.

Jimmy was always very careful not to favor the top prospects on his club. If he was running a drill, he wouldn't just involve the most highly regarded players on the club, he'd bring in other players so that he'd keep the loyalty of all his players. That's just the mark of a good baseball manager.

Jimmy Williams was always very careful not to favor the top prospects on his club. That's the mark of a good manager.

THE ROBINSONS

Frank Robinson and Brooks Robinson were two of the finest players I've ever been associated with. Frank was blessed with great natural talent. But he, like all the great ones, came out and worked at his job. If we were working on something as a group, he did it right and he urged others to do it right if they weren't. That's what you have to do to be a truly great player.

I'd put Frank up there with all the other all-time greats. He hit 586 home runs. He drove in more than 1,800 runs and he scored more than 1,800 runs. He hit for average—he was a lifetime .294 hitter—and he was just a great all-around player. In his six seasons in Baltimore, 1966–71, the Orioles won four pennants.

I can't say that Frank was the best player we had, or the best I've ever been around, or the best I ever saw, because we had Brooks and Boog Powell on those clubs, as well as Jim Palmer and Dave McNally and Mike Cuellar. There were a lot of great ballplayers in the big leagues at that time.

That's like asking, "Who was the best player who ever played the game?" Well, whoever you say you're going to get an argument. You could talk about Joe DiMaggio, he was a complete player, there wasn't any question about it. But then somebody's going to say, "Wait a minute, what about Willie Mays? What about Babe Ruth? Ted Williams? Stan Musial?" You're talking about a group of people that you can't narrow down to one person. You can have an opinion, but even though you might say your opinion is fact, that doesn't mean it is.

Frank Robinson came out and worked at his job. He did it right and he urged others to do it right if they weren't. That's what you have to do to be a truly great player.

The era that a particular player played in doesn't mean a whole lot. A good baseball player today would be a good player if he had played years ago. A good player of years ago would be a good player today. A good player is a good player. The type of player that someone is today, that's the type of player he's going to be wherever or whenever he plays. The fact that they played the game a little bit differently years ago doesn't take away from the individual player's ability.

Brooks Robinson was also a great player with tremendous natural ability. And Brooks took ground balls at third base every day. He practiced his job, and he practiced it correctly. Whenever I talk about Cal Jr. and Mark Belanger, I talk about how when they went out and took their ground balls, they took them correctly. They might have caught the ball one-handed, but they caught it properly. It was the same thing with Brooks. He went out and took his ground balls correctly, and when that same ground ball was hit in the game, it was automatic for him to approach it the right way.

Brooks wasn't blessed with a strong throwing arm, but he made up for the lack of velocity on his throws by getting rid of the ball quickly and being very accurate. He also had tremendous reflexes on hard-hit balls.

Brooks Robinson was a very intelligent player. You have to be intelligent if you want to be a good player, there's no question about that.

Brooks studied hitters and pitchers—he knew how to play each hitter, and he knew the type of pitch that was being thrown in a particular situation—so he was able to position himself better. That's being prepared to go out and play your game. He was a very intelligent player. You have to be intelligent if you want to be a good player, there's no question about that.

As I've said so many times, the defensive player has to be thinking: What am I going to do with the ball when it's hit to me? He goes over that before the play, before the pitch is made. As a player you have to do that consistently. That's how you become a good player.

The defensive player has to be thinking: What am I going to do with the ball when it's hit to me? He goes over that before the play, before the pitch is made.

PALMER'S PLANNING

Jim Palmer played for me in Aberdeen, South Dakota, in his first year in pro ball. He was the third starter on that club, and he always sat on the bench and studied the hitters in between his starts. For an eighteen-year-old kid coming into pro ball, that was quite unusual.

Usually an eighteen-year-old would pitch for a while before he would start to study the hitters, but Jim came into the game doing that, and he did that his whole career. That's one of the reasons why he won so many games—268 in nineteen seasons—and his career ERA in the big leagues was 2.86, which is just outstanding. He was also a guy who would welcome advice and suggested adjustments from his pitching coach.

Jim was very intelligent when he came into professional baseball, and that didn't change over his entire career. He had an idea of how he was going to pitch to the hitters on a ball club before he even took the mound. As a pitcher, that's one of the things that you have to do. It's a lot better when a pitcher does that, rather than putting an overall blanket on how he would pitch a hitter. Each pitcher's stuff is different, so one pitcher may be able to get a guy out with a fastball and another pitcher may have to get the same hitter out with a breaking ball.

Jim Palmer had an idea of how he was going to pitch to the hitters before he even took the mound. Each pitcher's stuff is different, so one pitcher may be able to get a guy out with a fastball and another pitcher may have to get the same hitter out with a breaking ball.

SCOUTING THINGS OUT

The only year I scouted for the Orioles was 1975. I started out in spring training that year with the major-league club as an instructor. Then, as spring training moved along, I began the scouting part of the job, which was primarily covering clubs in the American and National leagues. I was concentrating on the American League clubs with the idea of being able to see the talent in the league before joining the Orioles coaching staff the next year. I would have more knowledge of the American League because I would have had the opportunity to see the players firsthand and turn in my scouting reports.

Then Walter Youse left our organization and went with Harry Dalton to California. The Orioles asked me if I would take Walter's job, which was cross-checking. Cross-checking involves looking at the high school and college free agents. Not to confuse the term "free agent," as it's used today to refer to a veteran major leaguer whose contract is up, a free agent at that time was a young player who hadn't yet been signed, or hadn't even come into pro ball—in other words, a high school player, a college player, or a sandlot player.

Even though the amateur draft was in effect, a cross-checker was someone who would go see those players who had been classified by our free-agent scouts as upper fair, good, or excellent prospects. The cross-checker would go in and evaluate those players. He was getting more knowledge, and being more sure of that particular player in those higher classifications of prospects. When I was asked to do that I agreed, because I had never refused to do anything that I was asked to do. I did that for a little more than a month, because June is the draft. I was seeing those players in April and May, up to the draft time in June, and turning in reports on them.

Then after that was finished I took up the regular duties that I was going to have for that year: seeing the other American League clubs, and also doing a little bit of advance scouting for the major-league manager, Earl Weaver. In other words, I would go and see a club before the Orioles played them, and then give the major-league manager a report on what I saw on that club: Who's swinging the bat real well for them, who's pitching well, what are their tendencies, who's stealing bases, where does this guy hit the ball, where does that guy hit the ball, and that sort of thing. At other times I was just covering the various American League clubs, as well as six National League clubs, and evaluating each player.

Scouting is a fine job, but the best job in baseball is

playing. The next best job is being a manager or a coach, because you have the uniform on and you're out on the field. The next best job is being a scout, because you're still in the ballpark, but I prefer to have the uniform on and be on the field.

The Best Jobs in Baseball
1. Playing
2. Managing or coaching
3. Scouting

WHAT A SCOUT
LOOKS FOR

From my end of it, the professional end, you couldn't draft or sign a player until he was out of high school. There was no point in looking at a Little League player. Nobody's smart enough to project that far ahead anyhow.

So, when a guy is a senior, you start watching him to see how he does. Maybe you saw him as a junior, because you were there watching a senior on his team or another team the year before. When he was a junior you might have put a "follow" on him, which means, "I want to see this guy next year."

But up until that time there's no point in looking at the abilities of the younger players. Sure, you look at them and you say, "Here's a freshman, he has good arm strength, he has good hands," and that type of thing. But you don't really get serious about him until he's a junior or a senior.

The most difficult traits to evaluate in a young player aren't physical ones. They're heart and stomach—how hard a guy will work, how tough he is, and his level of desire. You can see the arm strength and the running ability, you can get an idea of his power, and you get a chance to see the fielding ability, but you don't know what's in the stomach and in the heart. Every young player is going to improve. But it's what's in that heart and what's in that stomach that determine how hard a particular player is going to work, and just how much he's going to improve.

> *The most difficult traits to evaluate in a young player are heart and stomach—how hard a guy will work, how tough he is, and his level of desire.*

From the scout's perspective, a lot of it is gut feeling. I'm sure there were players who I predicted would play in the big leagues, who didn't get there, I know that. They might have gotten outnumbered, though. It wasn't because of their talent, it was because of numbers—there were just too many good players in the system at that time. In other words, there might have been a guy at Double A who couldn't make the Triple A club because of the caliber of the players who were already there. If he had gotten the opportunity to play at the Triple A level at that time, he may have benefited and moved on to the major leagues. But by not getting the opportunity at the right time, he didn't get the chance to play in the big leagues. As a player, you need to be in the right place at the right time, and then you need to be ready to take advantage of that opportunity.

ON TO THE
COACHING RANKS

When I joined the Orioles' coaching staff in '76, I started out as the bullpen coach, replacing George Staller, who had retired after the previous season. Then when Billy Hunter left to take the Texas Rangers' managing job in June of '77, I became the Orioles' third base coach.

In the Baltimore organization at that time, the third base coach was also responsible for setting up and running the spring training program, and taking care of everything right up until game time, and then the manager would run the ball game. I was very familiar with all of that because I had run the spring training program in the minor leagues, and our major-league program and minor-league program were one and the same.

Earl Weaver, who was the major-league manager at the time, and I had worked in the minor leagues together—I had played for Earl one year, in '60, and we had managed in the minor leagues together. Earl knew what I could do as far as handling everything prior to gametime, and I just went out and did it every day.

We had a lot of outstanding baseball people in our organization in those days. When I was managing in the minor leagues, I don't think there was any place in our system you could look where there weren't people whom other major-league clubs wanted to acquire to manage or work in their organizations. If these men didn't move up to the big leagues as a coach or manager with Baltimore, they eventually did so with another organization.

Jim Frey and Joe Altobelli were in our minor leagues. George Bamberger was a pitching coach and George Staller was a manager in our minor leagues. Billy Hunter played and coached in the Baltimore organization at the major-league level. Every one of those men were Baltimore property, so to speak, even though they had played elsewhere before they joined the Orioles as instructors, coaches, or managers. Every one, save for Staller, went on to manage in the big leagues.

> *The Orioles had a solid system, and they had solid people running it.*

We had good instructors, too. Billy DeMars was in the Baltimore organization during that same period. Billy went on to coach third base for the Philadelphia Phillies, and he coached for thirteen years in their organization before moving on to Montreal and then Cincinnati. Vern Hoscheit was with us during that period, and he went on to coach for the Oakland Athletics and California Angels, and he was bullpen coach for the New York Mets for four years. Harry Dunlop was also with us in that period, managing in our system, before moving on to coach for a number of other big-league clubs, including the Royals, Reds, and Padres.

We had a number of outstanding baseball people who were together for seven years in the minor leagues during spring training, including DeMars, Hoscheit, Weaver, Frey, Altobelli, and myself. We weren't always together for those seven years, because at that time the Triple A club was separate: Rochester trained in Daytona Beach, away from the minor-league operations, which was Double A on down. Earl and Joe both managed at Rochester. But we were all working in the Orioles' minor-league system at that time, and we all helped set the tone for the organizational philosophy. That was the key: The Orioles had a solid system, and they had solid people running it.

There were other organizations that were very strict with fundamentals and had their set ways of doing things from top to bottom. At that time the Orioles were a good organization, an excellent organization, but we weren't the only good or excellent organization. There weren't many big-league clubs that had greater success than we did from 1966 to '83, though, when we won six American League pennants and three World Series.

STEADY EDDIE

Cal Jr. has talked often about the positive influence that Eddie Murray had on him during his career. Eddie was with the Orioles when Cal got there, in 1981, and they already knew one another through their association in spring training. Eddie had come up through the minor leagues with the Orioles. He played for me in the instructional league, where we allowed him to switch-hit, because that was something that Eddie wanted to do. I think it was a great thing for him. He worked at his job of hitting, fielding, and everything else, but Eddie was also blessed with great natural ability—he was just a very good hitter.

Eddie was criticized by a lot of people, but I always thought that he had very good work habits. He came out on the field, he did his work, and he was a very smart, heads-up player, and Cal respected Eddie and the way he went about things. I think that was the basis for Cal and Eddie's relationship—their approach to the game was similar in those respects. Then by '82 they were playing on the same club, and they just seemed to form a very close friendship. Eddie took Cal under his wing, but I think what they had was more a very good friendship, both on and off the field.

We stressed the fundamentals in the Baltimore organization. If we were doing rundown plays, Eddie Murray did them the right way. If we were doing pickoff plays, Eddie did them the right way. That's the only way to do something: the right way.

Here's an example of how Eddie was misunderstood: Sometimes when the pitching coach went to the mound to talk with a pitcher, Eddie would stand at first base with his arms folded. Well, people took exception to that, but I always said that standing with your arms folded is a very relaxed position, and I didn't see anything wrong with it.

Eddie worked at his job, and he was a good defensive first baseman. He picked balls very well around the bag at first base, and he was never given credit for that. We stressed the fundamentals so much in the Baltimore organization. If we were doing rundown plays, Eddie did them the right way. If we were doing pickoff plays, Eddie did them the right way. That's the only way to do something: the right way.

REGGIE'S CONFIDENCE

I had plenty of opportunity to observe Reggie Jackson in his twenty-one years in the big leagues, and Reggie played for the Orioles in 1976, the year I joined the coaching staff. Reggie was blessed with all the talent in the world. He could hit, he could run, he could throw, he could field, and he could hit for power. He liked to play the game, and he, like others on our club, worked very hard at his job. All Reggie wanted to do was go out and win.

Anyone who watched Reggie play could see that he had a tremendous amount of self-confidence, and confidence is the key to any area of the game. You have to have confidence to hit. You have to have confidence to field. You have to have confidence to do anything. And Reggie had confidence.

Unlike some people, I didn't think Reggie was a hot dog—not in any way. Reggie came to the park to give 100 percent and he went out and did that. The man hit 563 home runs in the big leagues and drove in more than 1,700 runs, so there's no way you can say that he didn't produce. I guess you could say that Reggie had a little flare about him, but he certainly wasn't what you would call a hot dog, not by any means.

Anyone who watched Reggie Jackson play could see that he had a tremendous amount of self-confidence, and confidence is the key to the game. You have to have confidence to hit. You have to have confidence to field. You have to have confidence to do anything.

THE EARL OF BALTIMORE

One of the great experiences of my career was playing and coaching for Earl Weaver in the Orioles organization. You couldn't ask for a better person to work for than Earl. I worked with him for a lot of years and enjoyed every minute of it.

What made Earl a successful manager? Well, he knew talent, he knew the game of baseball, and he utilized the strengths of his people. He knew how to handle a ball club and he commanded great respect because of his knowledge of the game.

Earl Weaver knew talent, he knew the game of baseball, and he utilized the strengths of his people. He knew how to handle a ball club and he commanded great respect because of his knowledge of the game.

The 1960s and '70s were a pretty good era for Baltimore. Everyone in the organization shared the same philosophy. There was a way to go about things, and we went about them that way. We were a better club for it, and we were going to win. From 1969 to '79, under Earl, the Orioles won six division titles and four pennants.

Working with Earl meant you studied the game. And I studied Earl Weaver as a manager when I was a coach under him. I watched the things that he did and it helped me become a better coach and a better manager. I guess if there was anything that I gained from Earl it was more of a desire to win than I already had—and I didn't think I could get any more of that. Earl just has an extraordinarily competitive mentality.

> *If there was anything I gained from Earl it was more of a desire to win than I already had—and I didn't think I could get any more of that. Earl just has an extraordinarily competitive mentality.*

TOUGH TIMES IN '87

The Orioles had a difficult year in 1987, my first year of managing in the big leagues, because we weren't blessed with a lot of talent, and we were essentially in a rebuilding situation. The idea was to help the club over the course of that winter, go into spring training in '88 and still try to improve the club with acquisitions and, if we were unsuccessful in doing that, we would continue trying to improve our club into the 1988 season.

In '87, after Billy was called up from Triple A to play second base, there was a lot made of the fact that I became the first major-league manager ever to have two sons play for him. Well, I never really thought of it that way. Having managed in the minor leagues for fourteen years, I saw so many young guys come along. I always said that when I was managing I was father to twenty-five players, not just one or two. So when I looked out at second base and shortstop, and saw those two out there, I saw just another pair of young guys out in the middle of the diamond—something that I was very accustomed to seeing in our organization. I never thought of it from the father's perspective. We had a good second baseman, we had a good shortstop. We had two young players who could do a lot of things. They could turn the double play as well as anybody. But I was just looking at them as two more young guys who were coming along in the Oriole system, as I had seen so many times before.

We knew going into the '87 season that we weren't a club that could compete with the good ball clubs. We knew it would be a struggle. Eddie Murray at first base and Cal Jr. at short were the only real MVP-type players we had. Pitching was a big problem: Nobody won more than ten games for us, and Dave Schmidt, at 10-5, was the only pitcher on the club to finish with a winning record. In the month of June alone we used nine different starting pitchers and eleven different relievers. We hit a lot of home runs that year—211, third-best in the major leagues—but we gave up a lot of home runs, too—226, more than any other team— and ended up at 67-95, the second-worst record in the American League.

I thought things were going to get better the next year. I had no idea that I was going to be fired after losing the first six games, because all winter long we had talked about the needs of our club: what we had to do in the winter, what we had to continue to do in spring training and into the '88 season. This was the idea going in, that we would continue to try to improve our ball club during the season, because it wasn't possible to do all the work prior to the start of the season, and

everyone knew that. Could things have worked out differently? Well, we'll never know the answer to that.

> *When I was managing I was*
> *father to twenty-five players,*
> *not just one or two. So when I*
> *looked out at second base and*
> *shortstop, I saw just another*
> *pair of young guys out in the*
> *middle of the diamond. I never*
> *thought of it from the father's*
> *perspective.*

A COMEBACK?

There was an idea that was floated in 1990 about the Orioles putting me on their active roster so that I could become the first father ever to play with two sons in a major-league game. This was the same year that the Seattle Mariners had Ken Griffey, Sr., and Ken Griffey, Jr., playing side-by-side in the same outfield, and the notion was that the Orioles could go that one better by having me behind the plate, with Cal at shortstop and Billy at second base.

I wasn't really ever approached about it directly, but the idea got a fair amount of attention after John Steadman came out in favor of it in a September 5th column in the *Baltimore Sun,* saying that the Orioles should activate me for one game after they were eliminated from the race for the American League East title.

I think after Steadman wrote it and then got a little feedback, he realized that maybe, as great an idea as it was on the promotional side—he was very gracious in saying that the "The Orioles should feel indebted to Cal Sr. and to his family"—it wasn't too good an idea in some other ways. The idea itself was fine, it was the way they would've had to go about it that wasn't proper.

Anyway, that was the rumor, but that was as far as it was going to go, because I was fifty-four years old at the time and I hadn't been in a game for a lot of years. I wasn't going to make a farce out of the game just so I could say that I played on the same field with my two sons. That's not the idea of the game. If I were playing on the club to help the club, where there was a need for me to be playing because of an injury or something, that would've been a different story.

Steadman's column quoted Orioles president Larry Lucchino as saying that I had told the club that if it happened, I "wanted to be assured of four at-bats, not just a token appearance." But I never said anything like that. If I had been in the kind of condition to get four at-bats, then I would've been in the proper condition to play in a ball game.

> *I wasn't going to make a farce out of the game just so I could say that I played on the same field with my two sons.*

WHAT'S IN A NUMBER?

I wore number 7 for most of my managing career in the minor leagues. There wasn't any special significance to it, it was just a number that I liked. The only year that I didn't wear number 7 was 1962, my second season as a manager, when I went back to Appleton, Wisconsin, where I had played two years before.

We had a clubhouse guy in Appleton, an older gentleman who had been there when I played there in '60, and he already had number 19 hanging up in my locker when I walked in. I didn't have the guts to say, "No, thanks, I don't really want it." So I wore number 19 that year.

Then when I came to the big leagues in 1976, Mark Belanger, who had been the Orioles' starting shortstop for eight years, had number 7. So I wore number 47.

The funny thing about Belanger was, when he played for me at Class A Aberdeen in the early '60s, he wanted number 7, but I said, "No, Mark, you can't have number 7, that's my number." Then when I came to the big leagues in '76 Mark told me, "I'll get even with you now. You can't have number 7, that's my number."

But then I went back to number 7 after Mark went to the Los Angeles Dodgers as a free agent in '81, and I was probably wrong for doing that. I probably should've stayed with number 47, because things went downhill after I went back to number 7. In '88 I got fired as manager, and then I came back in '89 as a coach, still wore number 7, and got fired again. I probably would've been better off if I had just stayed with number 47.

Things went downhill after I went back to number 7. In '88 I got fired as manager, and then I came back in '89 as a coach, still wore number 7, and got fired again. I probably would've been better off if I had just stayed with number 47.

CHAPTER *2*

PLAYING THE GAME

The Little Things

The game of baseball is made up of many little things. If we do all the little things right, then we'll never have a big thing to worry about.

A SIMPLE GAME

There are really only three things necessary to play the game of baseball: bats, balls, and people. I know, to be realistic we need a fourth thing—a glove—but we could play without it. Without any of the other three, though, we can't play.

So you see, baseball is just a simple little game played with a bat, a ball, and, usually, a glove. Then they put the human being in the game to use the three dumb animals. If that human being becomes a dumb animal, then we really have problems. He has to be the smart one and be able to handle the bat, the ball, the glove, and himself.

Baseball is just a simple little game played with a bat, a ball, and a glove. Then they put the human being in the game to use the three dumb animals. If that human being becomes a dumb animal, then we really have problems.

ALL THE WORLD'S
A FIELD . . .

Baseball is just a walk of life. The things that you do in life, you do in baseball, and the things that you do in baseball, you really do in life. Here's some important advice for a baseball player that can also be used by any person who wants to be successful in any walk of life:

○ **Get a quick first step:** If the first step is quick, the steps that follow will be likewise—and quicker.

○ **Play heads-up:** We play baseball on the ground, not with it. You can't play this game with your head down.

○ **Communicate:** Verbal communication is essential on a baseball field. By talking we can make the catch on an in-between fly ball, rather than watching that ball fall for a base hit as we stand looking at one another.

○ **Anticipate:** First, everyone on the field should want the ball hit to them. In preparation we should say to ourselves, "What am I going to do with the ball when it's hit to me? To my right? To my left and slowly?" By doing this we're prepared to make the correct play at all times. Physical errors are going to happen, but we must keep mental errors to a bare minimum.

○ **Adjust—and Readjust:** There are so many variables in the game of baseball, which therefore necessitate constant adjustments. And it's not just those that have to do with the game itself. There's the cold, the heat, the wind, the sun, the mud, and so forth. The more you play, the more you'll find the need to do both.

Baseball is just a walk of life. The things that you do in life, you do in baseball, and the things that you do in baseball, you really do in life.

GIVE IT TIME

Patience is a key virtue in playing the game of base-ball—particularly so in terms of making a change from the way you may currently be doing something. For example, if you change the way you grip the baseball, you must be patient until the grip feels comfortable. Anything new takes time for adjustment, and we must have patience to stay with it long enough to give it a good try and get results.

Remember, in baseball, as in life, there's something new to be learned every day.

Patience is a virtue in baseball. Anything new takes time for adjustment, and we must have patience to stay with it long enough to give it a good try and get results.

THE IDEAL HITTER

The ideal hitter would possess many qualities that would serve him well in life. Among them would be: strength, determination, coordination, confidence, vision, rhythm, style, body control, quick hands, and a willingness to learn and to take advice.

He would have a relaxed body and a loose, natural arm action. He would blend the important parts of hitting—bat and grip, stance, step or stride, swing, and follow-through into a smooth, graceful motion. While waiting for the pitch he would be perfectly relaxed, with his feet spread comfortably and his body turned toward the plate. Eyes, hips, and shoulders would be level, and the weight of his body would be distributed almost evenly on both feet. His bat would be back and ready.

He would watch the ball until it hit the bat. His swing would be clean, free, and crisp, and the ball would be struck out in front of the plate one to one-and-a-half feet in front of his body, with the full power of the shifting weight behind it. His body would follow through in the direction in which the ball was hit, and his bat would continue around under its own momentum to the rear of his body. At no stage of the swing would this batter's head jerk out of line. He would follow the course of the ball from the moment it left the pitcher's hand until it hit the bat and was on its way.

The ideal hitter would possess many qualities that would serve him well in life: strength, determination, coordination, confidence, vision, rhythm, style, body control, quick hands, and a willingness to learn and to take advice.

SLUMPS

Things aren't always what they seem in baseball. The bat is round. The ball is round. But they're always telling you: *Hit it square!* What happens when you can't? Next thing you know, you're in a slump.

Occasionally I'm asked what's the best way to get out of a batting slump. Well, that's kind of like asking me how to cure the common cold. There hasn't been a way devised yet to work out of a slump.

Things aren't always what they seem in baseball. The bat is round. The ball is round. But they're always telling you: Hit it square!

You can work extra, you can not work at all, it's just a matter of what takes place with slumps. The hitter forgets the basics and gets his mind confused. Then it's a matter of that mind getting relaxed again. Sometimes it works one way, sometimes it works another. Sometimes it doesn't work at all. The way the human body and its nervous system works, hitters will be going through slumps until hell freezes over. I don't think they'll ever stop.

What's the best way to get out of a batting slump? Well, that's kind of like asking me how to cure the common cold. There hasn't been a way devised yet.

BELIEVE IN YOURSELF

When Cal first went away to pro ball, he occasionally would call home when he was having a little problem at the plate. And I would ask, "Well, are you popping the ball up? Are you beating the ball into the ground? What are you doing with the ball?" He'd tell me and I'd make a suggestion one way or the other. Often he'd go out the next day and get a couple of hits, restoring his confidence.

> *If you're confident that you can do it, then you can do it. But in the game of baseball you're not going to go 4-for-4 every day. You're going to have some 0-fers.*

Confidence is the greatest thing in anything you do. If you're confident that you can do it, then you can do it. But in the game of baseball you're not going to go

4-for-4 every day. You're going to have some 0-fers. And when you get into a little bad streak, you can lose your confidence. It may not be until you go out and pop one out of the ballpark, or hit a couple of balls well, that you regain it.

It's the same thing that usually takes place when a young man first goes away to the pros. He loses his confidence a little bit, because things aren't going as well as he would like. Then it's a matter of restoring that confidence. A little pat on the back helps an awful lot.

WHY FRED LYNN
COULD MAKE THOSE
SPECTACULAR CATCHES

Work habits are extremely important in baseball. Look at all the great players, and I don't know of one you could name who didn't have very good work habits. Fred Lynn, for example, had excellent work habits. In spring training Freddie would go into the outfield during batting practice and run the pitchers out of centerfield. The hitters would be taking batting practice, and Freddie wanted to play those balls off the bat, because that's the same thing he would be doing in the game.

On a ball hit into the alley in batting practice, Freddie would go up against the fence—even run into the fence—to catch the ball. Well, when the game came along, and that same ball was hit, Freddie would catch it. I had writers and other people say to me, "You've gotta stop Freddie Lynn from running into the fence." I would say, "If you stop Freddie Lynn from running into the fence, you're taking part of his ability away."

Freddie would also make throws in from the outfield during batting practice to test the bounces off the infield. Not nearly enough players do that. Some go out into the outfield and test the footing, but not the other part of it, which is just as important.

For example, say it's the fifth inning of the ball game and somebody hits a ball to the centerfielder, and he has to make a play on it, and then throw it home to try to get a runner tagging up from third. What kind of hop is he going to get in front of home plate?

Often outfielders don't think about the second part of the play. They might be prepared for the first part of it, but there's not enough emphasis put on that phase of the game—studying the terrain—particularly for out-fielders. They go in the outfield during batting practice, and they might play the balls off the bat but they probably don't take into account some of the finer points that would help them, things that a Freddie Lynn would consider.

Outfielders sometimes don't get the opportunity before the game to make a throw to home plate, for example. If batting practice and infield were canceled, then that's a different story. But in that case, as a coach, I would inform the outfielders of the condition of the ground in front of home plate, saying something like, "The ground by home plate is very soft, so if you have a ball you've got to throw home, you're not going to get a skip on that ball. The ball's going to hit and die. You might even be better off on a particular ball making the throw all the way in the air." Those were things that we discussed, but the individual player today doesn't take those things into consideration enough.

Work habits. Practicing correctly. Perfect practice. It's so simple. Look at Brooks Robinson. He'd go out and take ground ball after ground ball, day after day after day. Cal would do the same thing. Bill would do the same thing. Mark Belanger, Richie Dauer, and Bobby Grich did the same thing. All of those guys—and I can keep naming them and naming them—had the proper work ethic and the work habits, and that's why they became great players. And that's why Freddie Lynn could make those catches.

On a ball hit into the alley in batting practice, Fred Lynn would go up against the fence— even run into the fence—to catch the ball. When the game came along, and that same ball was hit, Freddie would catch it.

THE DALKOWSKI EXPRESS

The hardest-throwing pitcher I ever saw was a left-hander named Steve Dalkowski, who played in the Orioles minor-league system in the late 1950s and early '60s. Ted Williams once said that of all the pitchers he ever saw—including Nolan Ryan, Bob Feller, and Sandy Koufax—Dalkowski was the fastest. I agree. There's no question in my mind.

If you were to take the radar gun that's used today and put it on Steve, I think it would've shown him to be throwing the ball somewhere in the neighborhood of 115 miles an hour. He was five-foot-ten, about 165 pounds, and his ball was light as a feather, because he threw all with the wrist. He wasn't wild inside or outside, he was just wild high: When his pitch was coming in, if it didn't look at first like it was going to hit your shin guards or hit home plate, then the ball would end up sailing over your head. His fastball would rise two feet—that's why if you were catching him you had to put your glove on the ground. If he was throwing it at the glove, you'd catch it belt-high. If he aimed it belt-high, it was over your head.

He threw the ball right out of the point of his shoulder, which was quite conducive to the ball going high. Paul Richards, who was the Orioles manager and a former big-league catcher, told him, "You've got to get your arm up. You can't throw from down there and be able to get the ball consistently over the plate." Well, Dalkowski then hurt his arm in '63 and he was never the same pitcher after that. He did develop a slider and he did some more pitching, but the velocity just wasn't there. After he hurt his arm he had better control, but he couldn't throw as hard.

Steve's release point was at shoulder-level. His fingers wouldn't be up above his head, or even up at the level of his head, like with most pitchers. That's the way he had always thrown. But in order to get the ball down in the strike zone you need to raise your arm higher. That's what Richards wanted him to do, but those muscles in his arm weren't used to being up there. As a result, he hurt the arm.

I don't think he would've been able to go to the big leagues with the type of delivery he had. That's why Richards changed him. But we'll never know how good he would've been. He once struck out Roger Maris on three pitches in a spring training game. He once pitched an inning of an exhibition game in Baltimore against Cincinnati. Birdie Tebbetts was the Reds manager at that time, and he told his hitters, "You go up to home plate, but don't you get in that batter's box close, because I don't want you hurt." But Steve could usually throw the ball over the plate—the problem was that it would be a head higher or more.

In a high school game in New Britain, Connecticut, Steve struck out twenty-seven batters in one game, and 313 in 154 innings for a season. (He also walked 180.) The Orioles signed him in 1957 for a $16,000 bonus, plus a car.

In one game at Aberdeen, South Dakota, he struck out eighteen and walked twenty-one. In a game in Wilson, North Carolina, in the Carolina League, Richards put a limit on him of 120 pitches. Steve left the game in the second inning. We were getting beat 11–0 and the bases were still loaded. He either walked them or he struck them out. In another game in Kingsport, Tennessee, he struck out twenty-four, walked seventeen, hit four batters, threw six wild pitches in a row, and lost 9–8.

As hard as Steve threw, if he'd have gotten to the big leagues he would've been a legend in his own time. I'm not too sure that he wasn't a legend in his own time anyhow. There are certainly plenty of stories about him. He supposedly broke one batter's arm with a fastball, and tore off another hitter's earlobe.

I caught Steve in the Carolina League, and I caught him in Pensacola, Florida. Steve didn't have good eyes, so as the catcher you'd put your hand on the right side of your leg to signal for a fastball, and your hand in the middle for a curveball. It was rare that you got the opportunity to call for a curveball with Steve, because he was never ahead in the count.

But one night in a game in Pensacola, we finally got ahead of the hitter, two strikes and no balls. So I gave

Dalkowski the curveball sign, which he didn't see, and instead he threw a fastball to this right-handed hitter. Some people said that the ball went off my glove, but it didn't even touch my glove, because I had the glove down on the ground. When Steve threw the fastball, it went over my right shoulder without me even touching it, hit the umpire in the mask, and broke it in three places. It sent the umpire to the hospital with a concussion.

That's the type of fastball Steve had—you weren't going to look for a curveball and come close to catching his fastball, particularly when your mind-set was to make him get the ball down, which meant you were going down very low with your target.

As hard as Steve Dalkowski threw, if he'd have gotten to the big leagues he would've been a legend in his own time.

VERSATILITY PAYS OFF

I always recognized and appreciated versatility in players, and it was also something I prided myself on every place I played. When I started in Phoenix in 1957 I was listed as a catcher, but I played a lot of games in the outfield. I also played a good bit of third base in the minor leagues. I recognized early on the value of being able to play more than one position, and oftentimes I was asked to play more than one spot in a game.

As a player I always felt that I could play anywhere on the field. If our ball club had somebody hurt or somebody sick, that never concerned me because I knew that I could go play that particular spot on the field. I understood the value of versatility even more when I began managing on the minor-league side and coaching and managing at the major-league level.

For a manager, a player who can play several positions is a very valuable commodity, particularly at the minor-league level. Years ago in the minor leagues, you had seventeen or eighteen players on your roster—and sometimes fewer than that. You didn't have five starting pitchers and seven guys in the bullpen. You carried eight pitchers—sometimes seven. With an eighteen- or seventeen-man roster, there wasn't a whole lot of room for extra pitchers or extra players. If you had, for example, nine regulars and eight pitchers, you had one extra regular player. One time when I was managing in Miami, when we were allowed to carry eighteen players, I had two regulars injured and I wound up with a third regular getting hurt in the game. I had to play a pitcher in the outfield to finish the ball game.

A guy who can play several positions is a very valuable commodity to a manager.

THE TOUGHEST
POSITION ON THE FIELD

People talk about catcher, shortstop, and centerfield as being the toughest and most demanding positions to play, but I don't look at it that way. People say, "The catcher's involved on every pitch," and "The shortstop's involved on every pitch because he has duties when a runner is stealing a base or when the hit-and-run is on," but any place you play on a baseball field you're involved on every pitch. It could be anything from catching the ball to making a relay throw to backing up a base, but at the very least it means being ready for when the ball is hit to you. I don't look at one position as being tougher than another.

You have demands at every position, whether it be third base or centerfield or leftfield. It's not just a matter of how many balls you have hit to you at a particular position.

Something else I find amusing is that oftentimes in baseball, a big guy has bad hands and the manager talks about playing him at first base. Well, at first base you have to handle the ball a whole lot more than you do at other positions, because you're taking the throws for the putout from the third baseman, from the short-stop, from the second baseman, and from the pitcher. If a guy has bad hands, I don't think you want to play him at first base.

You have demands at every position, whether it be third base or centerfield or leftfield. No matter what position you play, you're involved with every pitch.

THE IMPORTANCE
OF SELF-EVALUATION

I always felt that I had a good handle on my strengths and weaknesses as a player. That helped me make an adjustment to managing in the minor leagues, where the evaluation and grading of players is so important. I always felt that I could judge talent, and so I felt I could judge my own ability as well.

It's important for a player to have the ability to look at himself objectively. I'm not convinced that all players, as they move up the ladder and want to retain a job, can honestly say that they're looking at themselves clearly. But I do think that most players have the ability to do that—not necessarily kids coming into pro ball, but guys who have played a while. They see the talent on their own club, they see the talent in the league, so they should know where they stand in that group.

It's a fine line: You want to be confident, you want to believe in your abilities, and you don't want to sell yourself short. But at the same time you also don't want to overestimate what you can do. That doesn't help you.

When you get down to contracts, a player who has played a while says, "Well, I deserve this because I can do more than this guy did, or more than that guy did." Players have a tendency to say things like, "I was a .280 hitter at Double A, and that guy at Triple A at the same position was a .230 hitter." Well if that guy hasn't played Triple A, then he doesn't know how difficult it is to play at that level. He can't really make the comparison. He's only surmising. From that side of it, the player doesn't know how to evaluate himself, but the guy who's playing in that Triple A league knows in his own mind, and in his own heart, where he stacks up in that particular league.

> *You want to be confident, you want to believe in your abilities, and you don't want to sell yourself short. But at the same time, you also don't want to overestimate what you can do. That doesn't help you.*

HOW MUCH
CAN IT HURT?

When my boys were little, I used to hit grounders to them, and I always told them that the ball only weighs five-and-a-quarter ounces, so it's not going to hurt you. True, if the ball takes a very severe hop and bounces up and breaks your nose, that's going to hurt. But a broken nose really isn't that big a deal. You put it back in place and you go on.

I always told them that the ball wasn't going to hurt them, so that they'd stay aggressive both as hitters and as fielders. Yes, there are times when you want to get out of the way of the ball, like when a pitcher is throwing it ninety miles an hour at your head. That's no picnic, and it hurts, there isn't any question about that. It can do a lot of damage.

But basically, the ball *isn't* going to hurt you. You need not have any fear of the ball. Your eyesight and your reflexes are so quick that you can rely on them. When your eyes tell your brain the truth, you can get out of the way of being hurt. Everything we do in baseball we do out in front: We catch the ball out in front, we throw the ball out in front, and we hit the ball out in front. This is so the eyes can relay information to the fastest computer in the world—the human brain—and then that computer can get the rest of the body in the right place. When I was hitting ground balls to Cal and Bill and the ball would take a bad hop and hit them in the head or body, I would always say, "That ball can't hurt you. Come on, let's go again."

> *The ball isn't going to hurt you. You need not have any fear of the ball. It weighs only five-and-a-quarter ounces.*

When you go out on the field with that mind-set, you find that it doesn't hurt. There was a little kid over at the baseball school who once asked me, "How do you get over the fear of the ball hitting you?" I said, "Let the ball hit you. It won't hurt." Well, it so happened that it did hit him. In this particular game the third baseman made a wild throw as this kid was running to first base and the ball hit him in the shoulder. Well, it surprised him and shocked him, but then he realized that it wasn't so bad. That helped him get over his fear. You have to experience it to get over it. Like everything else, you've got to experience it before you know how it will feel.

When I tell the kids not to be afraid of the ball, I

speak from experience. One time in Boston during batting practice I got hit in the face with a line drive. Kiko Garcia was the hitter and I was throwing early batting practice. I threw a pitch down and away from him, and I said, "Kiko, you've got to get down and get that ball and drive it up the middle." The very next pitch I threw down in the same spot. He did as I told him and he drove the ball right up the middle. As I threw the ball, I came out from behind the protective screen and the ball hit me right between my nose and right eye. It hurt a lot, but I told myself that the ball only weighs five-and-a-quarter ounces.

Everything we do in baseball we do out in front: We catch the ball out in front, we throw the ball out in front, and we hit the ball out in front. This is so the eyes can relay information to the fastest computer in the world—the human brain—and then that computer can get the rest of the body in the right place.

I ended up coaching third base for that whole game, but I asked the TV people not to put the cameras on me because I hadn't been able to tell my wife about it yet. So they kept the cameras off me. But in a week I was healed up.

That's probably the worst shot I ever took, but in all my playing days I never had to go to the hospital. Recently I had to have an X ray and the doctor said, "I want to ask you about an injury to a bone in your right hip area. Tell me what happened there." I said, "I got hit with a line drive by Jim Fuller in Clearwater, Florida."

At the time of that incident, I was running an instructional club that trained in Clearwater. I was watching Fuller hit in the batting cage and I was walking out of the cage toward the dugout. I had a Coke in my hand and I went over to the end of the pitching machine where I could look in to get a better view. And, like Kiko Garcia, the pitch was down and away and I said, "Fuller, you've got to go down and get that ball and drive it up the middle." Well, the next pitch happened to be in the same spot and he went down and got it. He hit it back through a hole in the cage and I moved the Coke and it hit me on the right hip. Right away I knew the bone was broken.

Chico Fernandez was our infield instructor, and I told him, "You're coaching third base today." Of course, he didn't know what had happened. It took me twenty minutes to get from where I was hit to the dugout, about 90 feet away. I was supposed to play golf afterward and did. Doc Cole, our trainer, and I played. I told him, "You're driving the cart. You're going to drive as close as you can to the ball." Which he did, and I probably played one of the better rounds of golf that I've ever played because I couldn't get over on the right side, I had to stay on the left side. It worked out fine, though. After all, the ball weighs only five-and-a-quarter ounces.

WINTER WORKOUTS

The boys and I did a number of little drills when they were younger, to get ready for the season. You can do quite a bit indoors before spring arrives, and you don't need a whole lot of space. When the kids got a little bit bigger, and they'd outgrown the yard, I used to arrange to use the old high school gymnasium here in town.

I'd go down there in January and early February, when I wanted to throw the ball around to get my arm in shape before I went to spring training. I'd take the boys with me and they'd throw with me or they'd play catch, and in the process we'd hit the ball some.

I used to use the soft-toss drill with a net that I hung down from the stage curtain. The hitter would be about six or eight feet from the net. I'd be positioned fairly close to the net, but off to the side—not directly side-to-side with the hitter. I'd still be out in front of him, but I'd be off to the side so when I tossed the ball they'd step and hit it into the net and not back at me. You develop bat speed with the soft-toss drill. The tee-ball drill—simply putting the ball on a tee and hitting it—is very good, too.

We'd also hit ground balls in the gym. This was a small gymnasium, not a large gym like a lot of high schools have today. I would get on one end of the gym with a fungo bat and hit balls to the boys. I'd start out hitting the ball straight at them, then I'd hit the ball to their left and to their right, and they'd work on their first step, or their crossover step, in going after the ball. That's a little drill that's very good. You can do it out on a baseball field, too. You don't have to put the fungo hitter all the way at home plate and put a guy all the way out at deep shortstop. You can put the infielder in the middle between first and second or between second and third, and the fungo hitter can stand forty or fifty feet away. Naturally, you're not going to hit the ball really hard, but you're going to hit it hard enough so that the fielders have to move for it.

The boys and I did a number of little drills when they were younger, to get ready for the season. You can do quite a bit indoors before spring arrives, and you don't need a whole lot of space.

COLLEGE BASEBALL VERSUS
THE MINOR LEAGUES

After I graduated from high school in 1953, I had a chance to attend Washington College in Chestertown, Maryland, but I decided not to accept the soccer scholarship they offered me because I wanted to play pro baseball. Today, even though a lot has changed since then in terms of the level of play in college baseball, I would recommend to any young person who's interested in playing in the major leagues to go straight into professional baseball out of high school, rather than go to college and play.

I know that a lot of people disagree with what I'm saying, and I do realize the importance of a good education. But if you really have your heart set on playing in the big leagues, the best way to get there is via the minor-league route. There are four main levels of play in the minor leagues, and the caliber of play at each level is higher than that of the previous level. If a major-league club drafts a high school player, it has a chance to develop his skills a whole lot better than a college team would. The professional club can bring the young guy along much quicker.

In college the quality of play is going to stay pretty much the same every year of his four years there. So when he comes out of college he's not as prepared to play in the big leagues as someone who's played in the minors for four years.

> *I would recommend to any young guy who's interested in playing in the major leagues to go straight into professional baseball out of high school, rather than go to college and play. The caliber of play at each level of the minor leagues is higher than that of the previous level. In college the quality of play is going to stay pretty much the same every year.*

Over the years it's become apparent that it's much harder to make an impact in baseball right out of college or high school than it is in professional football and basketball. Besides the obvious fact that the colleges are, in effect, the farm systems for pro football and pro basketball, the reason for this, I believe, is that the skills it takes to play baseball are much greater and much harder to develop than the skills required in football and basketball.

Take an everyday player in baseball. He's got to catch, throw, hit, field, and run. Hitting a baseball alone is extremely difficult. You've got to walk up to home plate and be able to hit fastballs, curveballs, change-ups, sliders, and so forth. On the other hand, a defensive back in football only has to worry about covering a receiver. An offensive lineman only has to block. So, it's easier for them to develop their skills and go right into the major leagues of football. The same is true in basketball.

Young athletes are aware of how hard it is to be successful in baseball. That's one of the reasons why the best athletes sometimes turn to basketball and football. Plus, some players—and even some college underclassmen and high school players—get bigger contracts quicker in pro football and pro basketball than they do in baseball. Years ago, when you came out of high school, baseball was the only sport that gave you the opportunity to make money as an athlete. You went into the minor leagues and you earned three or four hundred dollars a month. (In 1957, when I broke in to professional ball, I managed to get a contract for $400 a month at the Class C level, and meal money was $3 a day while on the road.) Players weren't coming out of high school into the NBA, or leaving college after a couple years to enter the NFL. They had to go to college in order to play pro basketball or pro football, if that's what they wanted to do.

No one had the chance to make $80,000 a year in those other sports, like Babe Ruth was making in baseball. Baseball was the sport that gave you the opportunity to make money. That was true for me. I had that little scholarship to go to Washington College and play soccer, but there was no professional soccer league available for me to join to make money after college. I loved the game of soccer and I was probably a better soccer player than I was a baseball player. If I could've made the kind of money in soccer that I could make in baseball, then I might have chosen soccer. But the opportunities just weren't there, so I decided to play baseball instead, and have never regretted it.

The skills it takes to play baseball are much greater and much harder to develop than the skills required in football and basketball.

WEIGHTY MATTERS

Years ago, when I was playing ball, nobody lifted weights. Most of the guys who made it to the big leagues had grown up on farms or in the countryside, and had spent their youth throwing hay around with pitch forks and milking cows by hand. This physical labor made them strong—this was weightlifting before weightlifting became a sport unto itself.

As baseball gained more popularity in urban areas, players from these areas started making it to the big leagues, and they didn't have the benefit of growing up working outdoors, so weight programs became necessary. The best programs aim at improving the strength of a player's hands, forearms, and wrists—areas where you have to be strong in order to succeed in baseball. Then of course, there's Mark McGwire—I think he thinks he has to have great, strong everything, including his little finger.

A baseball workout doesn't have to be complicated. You want to strengthen your arm? Throw the ball. That's what Cal has always done to keep his throwing arm strong. Want to strengthen your legs? Run. The best exercises are throwing a ball, hitting a ball, and catching a ball. To hit, you use your hands, wrists, and forearms the most. Boog Powell muscled the ball out of the park. Hank Aaron and Ernie Banks wristed the ball out of the park.

Since players have to have some strength all over the body, a general workout program is good for all. The best players take care of themselves year-round; weight training and working out never ends. With the schedule today being so demanding, players can't come to spring training to get in shape. They need to be in pretty good shape when they get there, and have to take care of themselves in the off-season, too. That didn't used to be the case; years ago, players did come to spring training to get in shape. They had to work during the wintertime to supplement their salaries. I don't think any of today's players have to do that, but they do have to take care of themselves and keep themselves in shape.

For years, the Orioles had a basketball team in the off-season. They played games against the faculties of various schools to raise money for the schools. It evolved into such a popular thing that eventually other groups were lining up to play the team. This was great for a while, but then the games got so rough that they had to quit playing for fear that someone would get hurt.

So Cal Jr., who loves to play basketball, and some of the other players started to play at the gym at his house. The Orioles aren't completely enthusiastic about this, but they know that if the players don't play there, they'll play someplace else. It gives them a workout, and it helps the Orioles club, because they've got players who are keeping themselves in better shape and building some camaraderie off the field.

A baseball workout doesn't have to be complicated. You want to strengthen your arm? Throw the ball. Want to strengthen your legs? Run. The best exercises are throwing a ball, hitting a ball, and catching a ball.

HOMER-HAPPY IN '98

The 1998 season was an incredible one for baseball. The Yankees put together one of the best seasons in history. David Wells captivated everyone with his perfect game. And, of course, Mark McGwire and Sammy Sosa thrilled us all with their great home run chase. Of all that transpired in 1998, I believe it was McGwire and Sosa who did the most for baseball. People became fascinated with the home run.

Some baseball purists have argued that the home run chase will ultimately be bad for baseball, that it has placed undue emphasis on the long ball at the expense of all other areas of the game, and has taught the lesson to young players that a home run is more important than a single. Well, I don't buy that. What the home run race did was bring people to the park to see a ball game. Maybe they came to see a home run, but by the same token they also saw and maybe learned to appreciate other facets of the game. They might say, "Well, there's better pitching in this game, so maybe there aren't going to be many home runs today. Let's see what this is all about." I think it's good for the game. Anything that's positive is good for the game, and to me this is a positive thing.

> *What the home run race did was bring people to the park to see a ball game. Maybe they came to see a home run, but by the same token they also saw and maybe learned to appreciate other facets of the game.*

As for the idea that young players are being taught to focus on hitting home runs, the mission of Little League and the youth leagues is to teach the fundamentals of hitting, which means to teach kids to make good solid contact with the ball. The idea is to generate bat speed and hit the ball hard somewhere. Home runs will take care of themselves.

The difference between a home run and a line drive

is an eighth of an inch on the bat, one grain on the bat. So, that's the thing that has to be—and I believe still is—taught in Little League and in the youth leagues: the correct fundamentals of hitting. Home runs will take care of themselves.

As for Little League and the youth leagues, the idea is to teach the fundamentals of hitting, which means to teach the kids to make good solid contact with the ball.

THE MYTH
OF THE JUICED BALL

Let's clarify one thing regarding all these home runs:
The ball is not juiced. Mark McGwire and Sammy Sosa
are so strong and they generate so much bat speed that
hitting home runs almost comes naturally to them.

Remember, Hank Aaron and Ernie Banks were not
big men, but they generated bat speed when they hit
home runs, just like McGwire and Sosa do. When people
talk about golf and hitting the ball a great distance,
what do they constantly refer to? Club head speed.
Well, it's the same thing in baseball. The club speed
makes the difference.

I've always told hitters, You don't have to be six-
feet-eight, 400 pounds. Simply put, it's the speed of the
ball against the speed of the bat that generates power.
A strong guy like McGwire gets that bat head going and
it comes flying through the hitting zone. When it makes
contact with that ball, the ball just flies.

It's a simple formula, one that has applied to baseball ever since the game was created. Hank Aaron and Reggie Jackson hit long home runs. Frank Robinson hit a ball out of Memorial Stadium. Mickey Mantle hit the ball over the hedge in Memorial Stadium before they had a centerfield fence out there. This phenomenon has been around for a long time.

The ball is not juiced. Mark McGwire and Sammy Sosa are just so strong and generate so much bat speed that hitting home runs almost comes naturally to them.

A FEMALE
MAJOR LEAGUER?

I may not see it in my lifetime, but I think the possibility is there for a woman to play in the major leagues. The opportunity is far greater today than it has ever been.

A lot of people might not agree with that statement, but a few years back, who would've agreed that women would be playing college baseball? Who would've agreed that there would be women playing semipro ball, or in the professional ranks in the minor leagues, as Ila Borders, a lefthanded pitcher, has done for the past couple of years in the Northern League?

The female athlete keeps getting better all the time. Take a look at those young women playing soccer at the college and national team levels. I thoroughly enjoy watching women's soccer because of the tremendous skills they display.

Of course, it's not just the female athlete who keeps getting better and better, and bigger and stronger. It's happening with athletes across the board. A six-foot-four-inch guy in basketball used to be a tall guy. Now he's a point guard. Strength would be the thing that could be most detrimental to a woman playing in the big leagues, but some of those young women, they're pretty strong.

Centerfield would be one possible position for a female player, because even though you want a center-fielder to have a good arm, if you look around the major leagues today, how many centerfielders can you find with good arms? Not too many. Certainly fewer have one than don't.

> *I think the possibility is there for a woman to play in the major leagues. The opportunity is far greater today than it ever has been. The female athlete keeps getting better all the time.*

I'm not cutting the female athlete down by saying that she's not as strong as the male athlete. She is in some respects. She may not be as strong as the strongest male athlete, but she's stronger than some male athletes. She can still be ranked as having a good arm, or an above-average arm, on the same scale with the male athlete.

To me, there's only one way that you judge ability.

You judge it on the major-league standard of excellent, good, fair, or poor. That's with respect to the major-league level. So if I tell you that the player in centerfield for Buffalo in 1998 has a good arm, I'm telling you that he has a good major-league arm. That's the only way that you grade.

You grade the male or the female exactly the same way. You're going to have some who will fall by the way-side, both male and female. But the female athletes are getting bigger, stronger, and better. Nobody out there can dispute me on that.

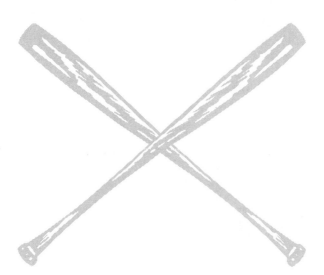

CHAPTER 3

THE IRON MAN

Cal's Legacy

Obviously, I'm very proud of Cal's consecutive games streak, but I hope it doesn't overshadow the numbers he's put on the board during his career. He's close to 3,000 hits and 400 home runs—he could reach both of those in the 1999 season. He has 1,500 RBIs and 1,500 runs scored. And don't forget, he has a tremendous fielding record at shortstop. In fact, if you look at statistics like assists and total chances, I think it's fair to say that Cal was as good a shortstop as there has ever been in the game.

CAL THE COMPETITOR

Cal has always had a very competitive nature, even when he was a boy. He always wanted to win at all costs, no matter what the game was—card games like canasta and hearts, jacks, table tennis, and Monopoly (when no one was looking, he'd steal $500 bills out of the bank)—on the playground, on the ball field, wherever. At bedtime on the road, Vi would promise a penny to the quietest child in order to get the kids to sleep. Well, Cal won all those, too—and he kept the pennies. Of course, he's always been that way about baseball, too. He always loved the thrill of the big pitcher-hitter confrontation.

I don't know if I can say that Cal is more competitive than I am, though. If, for example, I were to come out and say that he was more competitive in a card game than I was, I would probably get a lot of static from my wife and other people. So I can't say that. But he was always very, very competitive.

Earl Weaver was the same way. It didn't make a difference if you were playing baseball, or a pickup game of basketball, or cards. Whatever he was playing, he wanted to win. But in the case of both men, I'm talking about people who were very successful at the highest level. That ultra-competitive spirit is something you just have to have to succeed.

> *Cal has always had a very competitive nature, even when he was a boy. He wanted to win at all costs, no matter what the game was. That ultra-competitive spirit is something you just have to have to succeed.*

TALKIN' BASEBALL

When Cal was young, he'd ride along in the car with me to the ballpark. On most every ride, we talked baseball: fundamentals, strategy, trends, techniques—basically, we talked about anything that had to do with baseball. At the time, I didn't really realize how much of an impact it had on him.

Cal has often talked about how much he enjoyed those car rides, and how baseball provided a means for the two of us to be together. I can understand and appreciate how he felt about our baseball conversations and how they were a learning process for him. It obviously helped us draw closer as father and son, too. I was the best man at Cal's wedding, which I guess is kind of rare, to have the groom's father as the best man, but I was very proud and happy to do it. That's quite an honor.

There was a lot of baseball talk around our house, too. I can't say that we would sit down at the dinner table and make a particular point of discussing baseball. But if something happened to come up, we'd talk about it. If I couldn't talk baseball, I couldn't talk, because I didn't know anything else.

As far as our chats in the car, I guess it was a little bit like riding the bus in the minor leagues. I always said there was as much baseball learned on the bus as there was on the field. Often on bus trips when I was managing in the minor leagues, I'd sit on the arm of a chair three or four seats back from the front seat and I'd talk baseball with the players for two or three hours. We'd wind up with the whole ball club at the center of the bus, sitting on the arms of the chairs and talking about the game. It was great.

When Cal was young, he'd ride along in the car with me to the ballpark. We talked baseball: fundamentals, strategy, trends, techniques. It was a little bit like riding the bus in the minor leagues. I always said there was as much baseball learned on the bus as there was on the field.

I was fortunate. I always had good clubs in the minor leagues and guys who had ability. They were interested in learning, too, so it was an opportunity for everyone to learn.

> *If I couldn't talk baseball, I couldn't talk, because I didn't know anything else.*

HONOR STUDENT

One year when I was coaching in Baltimore, and Cal was in high school, the Orioles happened to have an eight o'clock game. It was a Friday night, national TV game, and the late start allowed me to go to the ballpark a half-hour later than normal. So I was able to see four innings of one of Cal's high school games, of which I usually saw very little.

Cal knew that when I came to his games I was going to be leaving early. I always stationed myself away from the grandstand, then when I'd leave to go to work, I'd whistle to catch him coming off the field, wave, and say, "See you later."

In this particular game Cal made a great play at shortstop: Backhanded a ball, came up over the top and threw the guy out at first base. I was leaving at the end of that inning, so I whistled over to him, and said, "I've gotta go. I'll see you later. By the way, where'd you learn to make a play like that?" He said, "You told me." I said, "I don't recall doing that. But I'll talk to you later about it." The next day I said, "Where did I teach you to make a play like that?" He said, "Well, do you remember the clinic in Rochester? That's the way you instructed the infielders to make that play."

Even though I hadn't felt that I was personally instructing Cal at that clinic, I guess I was in a way. Because he had been at the clinic and had paid attention, and then he had gone out and executed it.

"By the way," I asked Cal, "where'd you learn to make a play like that?" He said, "You told me."

THE TOUGHEST
ADJUSTMENT IN BASEBALL

The only time that Cal really struggled in baseball was when he initially went away to pro ball at age seventeen. That's the toughest adjustment a player has to make: going from high school—or even college or the sandlot—into professional baseball. In his first year in the minor leagues, with the Orioles' Rookie League team in Bluefield, West Virginia, Cal hit just .264 with no home runs in 239 at bats.

He didn't know what to expect. He'd come from an area where he had been a pretty good player. Now he was joining other players of that same classification, who were coming from their own areas where they'd been pretty good players. Any young man who goes into professional baseball has a lot of adjustments to make, and those adjustments take time. In baseball—in life—you have to do two things: adjust and readjust. You constantly have to do those two things.

In baseball— in life—you have to do two things: adjust and readjust. You constantly have to do those two things.

When Cal first went away, he was on a club that had some college players who were older and more experienced. He naturally wondered, "Am I in the right place? Can I do this?" When a young man first goes into professional baseball, naturally he feels he has pretty good ability or he knows he wouldn't have been signed. But when he gets there and sees other people—so many other people—with this same kind of ability, maybe even some with more ability, he questions himself a little bit. But then, eventually, he says, "Well, wait a minute. I can do these things. That's why I'm here." Then he starts to relax, clear his mind, and he goes out and makes the adjustment and does the things he's capable of doing.

After Cal got his feet on the ground, everything moved along very well: He raised his batting average to

.303 at Class A Miami in his second year. Sometimes that's very difficult to do, but that's the adjustment that has to be made. The toughest adjustment in baseball is the one going from the amateur ranks to the professional ranks, and the next toughest one is from the minor leagues to the major leagues.

When a young man first goes into professional baseball, naturally he feels he has pretty good ability or he knows he wouldn't have been signed. But when he gets there and sees so many other people with this same kind of ability, maybe even some with more ability, he questions himself a little bit. But then, eventually, he says, "Well, wait a minute. I can do these things. That's why I'm here."

THE WORK ETHIC

People often ask me if Cal gets his work ethic from me. I certainly can't take full credit for Cal's iron will—his mother had more than a little to do with that—but during my career as a player, manager, coach, and scout, I didn't make a habit of taking days off either.

As a player, there were times that I wasn't in the lineup because the manager decided somebody else was going to be in, but it wasn't because I didn't want to be in there. Whether if I was in the game or not, I was always in tune with the action that was unfolding on the field. One of the lessons I tried to teach my children was that, no matter what you're doing, stay focused at all times and you'll be a step ahead of the competition.

I'd probably be the world's worst fan, because if I'm not participating I don't have too much interest. That's why I've always been an active participant and why I've never been big on taking days off. No matter how sick or tired I am, simply participating is better than staying at home.

Whether I was in the game or not, I was always in tune with the action that was unfolding on the field. One of the lessons I tried to teach my children was that, no matter what you're doing, stay focused at all times and you'll be a step ahead of the competition.

In fact, there were many times when I was playing amateur ball that I caught three straight doubleheaders. It happened during tournament play. The format of these tournaments was that if you win, you play again right away. Sometimes they go on and on. Catching three straight doubleheaders is not hard. I caught four games one day in a tournament. I thought of it as just doing my job.

Once in the minor leagues, after I had caught two straight doubleheaders and the first game of a third in Cedar Rapids, Earl Weaver, my manager at the time, didn't start me for the second game. Well, I was very unhappy, and Earl knew it, because I wasn't in the lineup. I wound up pinch-hitting in the seventh inning of that game, so I did hit in all three doubleheaders.

I've never been big on taking days off. No matter how sick or tired I am, simply participating is better than staying at home.

BREAKING THE MOLD

When Cal first started playing shortstop at the major-league level, a lot of people speculated that he was too big to play the position, that he didn't fit the traditional mold of a shortstop. Well, I didn't believe in molds.

Traditionally, a manager would have his first and third baseman supply the power; his leftfielder and rightfielder would be power, run-producing guys; his centerfielder would be someone who could get on base and make the plays in the outfield; his second basemen and shortstop would be his defensive stars; and his catcher would be a guy who could drive in, and produce, runs.

Ballplayers today, in general, are bigger than they were years ago. Today there are probably only a couple of guys who wouldn't hit their head on the top of the dugout at Detroit's Tiger Stadium, and those would be the old coaches. Because you go back to the early- and mid-1900s, and five feet ten, five feet eleven was a tall guy. There were a lot of guys who were five six, five seven, especially shortstops. Luis Aparicio of the White

Sox and Willie Miranda of the Orioles were both under five ten. Albie Pearson of the Angels was five five.

So, in this conventional way of putting together a lineup, there were only three places for the little guy to play: shortstop, second base, and centerfield. But I say if a guy can play, he can play, no matter what his size. There's no reason that you can't have a big third baseman, a big shortstop, a big centerfielder, or a big second baseman. Obviously, Cal's success at shortstop proved that.

A lot of people say that Cal was the first big shortstop, but Marty Marion, who played for the St. Louis Cardinals in the '40s and '50s, was a pretty tall man. He was six two, had a career batting average of .263, and played some solid defense. Marion was considered big for a shortstop at that time, but there just isn't any pattern or standard criteria that you can use when you're setting up your ball club. You set up your club so that you can make the plays defensively, without worrying about molds as far as the size of people. If you've got a guy of Cal's size who has the ability to play solid defense and can give you power on offense, then why not play him at shortstop?

There were a lot of people who thought Cal would never be an everyday shortstop in the major leagues, but he had decided pretty early on that that was the position he wanted to play. He had caught a bit in Little League, as did Bill—I guess in a way they were trying to take after me—but they were both interested in other positions. I certainly wasn't going to force them to be catchers, and there was never a situation in which their coaches were forced to use them at catcher.

The thing that most people don't remember, or even know, is that in 1978, when Cal was seventeen years old, every major-league club had him projected as a pitcher. A lot of scouts thought he couldn't hit well enough to be an every-day player—even though he had batted .492 as a senior—and they were more intrigued by his arm: He was 7-2 as a senior with a 0.70 ERA while striking out one hundred batters in sixty innings, and he had thrown a two-hitter with seventeen strikeouts to win the Maryland Class A championship game.

Well, the Orioles drafted Cal with the forty-eighth pick that year, and even then the opinions were divided on where to play him: pitcher, shortstop, or third base. My feeling was, if he wants to be an infielder, let him try it. He can always move back to the mound down the road if things don't work out. Earl Weaver, who would ultimately be the guy who made Cal the Orioles' regular shortstop in 1982—agreed with me. But I guess if another club had drafted Cal, he might very well be pitching today.

If you've got a guy of Cal's size who has the ability to play solid defense and can give you power on offense, then why not play him at shortstop?

ENDING THE
CONSECUTIVE INNINGS
STREAK

Back on September 14, 1987, when I was managing the Orioles, I made the decision to end Cal's consecutive innings streak at 8,243, a streak that had spanned 904 games. We were in Toronto and our next two series were going to be on the road in Boston and New York. It was the bottom of the eighth inning of a game that we were losing 18–3, so I thought the time was right.

In the top of the eighth inning I told Cal, "If you hit this inning, then you're going to come out." He did hit, and grounded into a fielder's choice. Then he just looked at me and said, "All right." And I sent Ron Washington in to play shortstop.

I had been watching Cal closely in the locker room for two weeks prior to that, and the poor guy could barely get dressed. He was having to hurry to get out onto the field because he was being hounded so much by the media. So that day in Toronto I said to myself, It's time to give the guy a break. It's time to let him be able to come to the ballpark and get dressed and relax a little bit before he has to hurry out on the field.

When I made the decision, I thought it was the right one for Cal and for the team, so I didn't discuss it with Cal beforehand. It was a team decision, and Cal accepted it as one. When you're a player, your ultimate obligation is to your team and to your teammates. Cal recognized that, and so he wasn't upset that I pulled him out of the game early.

> *When you're a player, your ultimate obligation is to your team and to your teammates. Cal recognized that.*

Don't get me wrong: Cal objected a little bit. Any ballplayer who loves the game wants to be out there competing all the time. But Cal never questioned the decision. It was a player–manager thing, and he didn't question the manager. That's an area in which the media was unfairly critical of Cal, in suggesting that he controlled the Streak. That's just not true. He's always respected the managers he's played for and the decisions they made for the good of the team.

The media was unfairly critical of Cal in suggesting that he controlled the Streak. That's just not true. He's always respected the managers he's played for and the decisions they made for the good of the team.

When I was managing the Orioles and Cal was playing for me, I never looked at individual stats. Everything I did was team-oriented. When I wrote out that lineup card before each game, I put Cal's name in there because I believed that I had a better chance to win the game with him in there than without him.

He might make a key play at shortstop, he might turn a double-play. He might make a great defensive play to save a run. He might hit a home run. He might get a base hit to drive in the game-winning or -tying run.

There are so many things that a player like that can do to help win a ball game. You want those players in your lineup. It didn't have anything to do with preserving the Streak. I'd like to think that every manager for whom Cal played during the Streak acted the same way.

When I wrote out that lineup card before each game, I put Cal's name in there because I believed that I had a better chance to win the game with him in there than without him. It didn't have anything to do with preserving the Streak. I'd like to think that every manager for whom Cal played during the Streak acted the same way.

I like people who come to the ballpark to play, because that's the way I was as a player. I came to the ballpark to play a ball game and help my team. I didn't come to sit on the bench—I never gave any thought to that. And when the game is over, you need to be prepared to play the next day. That's how you go about doing your job, and that's what you want your people to do. What makes Cal so special is that he just has a tremendous desire to play the game. I was the same way as a player. I guess you could say that's the Ripken Way.

> *What makes Cal so special is that he just has a tremendous desire to play the game. I was the same way as a player. I came to the ballpark to play a ball game and help my team. I didn't come to sit on the bench.*

MY GREATEST MOMENT
IN BASEBALL

On the afternoon of September 6, 1995, my wife and I drove to Baltimore to watch Cal make history by breaking Lou Gehrig's record of 2,130 consecutive games. The atmosphere that night at Camden Yards was more electric than any World Series game I've ever attended. In fact, it made a World Series game feel like an exhibition game in spring training. That's how large all of this was. To be in that stadium, and to see, hear, and feel what was happening, well, I knew I was in the presence of something special.

I say it was bigger than a World Series game because of the emotion, the noise level, the hype, everything—it was just indescribable. I expected the atmosphere to be charged that night, but I didn't expect to be blown away by it. I had watched a lot of Cal's games on TV leading up to the record night, so I could get a picture of what would happen when he actually broke Gehrig's record. But what I experienced you could not possibly have pictured ahead of time.

Perhaps the most impressive thing to me, though, was how Cal handled himself on such a grand stage. I don't know anyone who could have handled it better. To be able to stay focused in that game was miraculous. And Cal homered on three straight nights: the night before he tied the record, the night he tied it, and the night he broke it.

> *The atmosphere that night at Camden Yards made a World Series game feel like an exhibition game. I don't know of anything that could top that night.*

Then again, Cal has always had the ability to rise to the occasion. That's a characteristic of a great player. He's also a very analytical player. He's always thinking—what am I going to do with the ball when it's hit to me? He knows what he's going to do with it. He knows what should be done in every situation. He's got an ability to filter out all the extraneous stuff and zero in on playing, even at a time like that.

He did let himself enjoy it, though. He took that famous lap around the stadium when the game became official. Rafael Palmeiro pushed him out there and said, "We're never going to get the game started again unless you get out there." I could tell Cal was having a great time, just reveling in the night and shaking hands with the fans, but I remember I leaned over to a friend as this was going on and told him, "They really should give him a golf cart. He's still got half of a game to play."

I've been asked many times, "What is your greatest moment in baseball?" Before that night I would always say, "I haven't had it yet." Well, I had to speak at a parade in my hometown of Aberdeen, Maryland, after the night of 2,131, and when I got up to talk I said, "I've had my greatest moment in baseball." I don't know of anything that could top that night. There hasn't been anything to top it so far and I can't visualize anything in baseball that would top it.

Cal has always had the ability to rise to the occasion. That's a characteristic of a great player. He's got an ability to filter out all the extraneous stuff and zero in on playing, even at a time like that.

THE SAVIOR?

A lot of people have called Cal the savior, the person who saved baseball, the person who brought back fans who had been turned off of the game ever since the 1994 strike. I don't buy that. I don't think baseball was as bad off as people tried to make it out to be. Sure, Cal's accomplishments and the way he handles himself and reaches out to the fans have been great for the game, but to say that he saved baseball is just an exaggeration.

> *A lot of people have called Cal the savior of baseball. I don't buy that. First of all, I don't think baseball was as bad off as people tried to make it out to be.*

I think some people are looking for excuses to say that people are down on baseball. Maybe initially after the '94 strike the fans were a bit slow to come back, but it seems to me that people have come back to baseball.

I don't think Mark McGwire and Sammy Sosa saved baseball in 1998, either. True, they both helped draw more people to the ballparks, especially later in the season, but attendance was already fairly high. They simply added to it. It never hurts to have somebody around that people can call a savior—a Cal Ripken, a Mark McGwire, or a Sammy Sosa—but it's not like the game has to have one. You can't hang it on one guy, anyway. Baseball will endure because of the game itself—not because of any one individual who's playing it.

> *It never hurts to have somebody like a Cal Ripken, a Mark McGwire, or a Sammy Sosa, but it's not like the game has to have a savior. You can't hang it on one guy, anyway. Baseball will endure because of the game itself—not because of any one individual who's playing it.*

FROM SHORT TO THIRD

Before the 1997 season the Orioles asked Cal to switch positions, from shortstop to third base. Even for someone as talented as Cal, changing positions is a difficult thing to do at the major-league level. He had a little trouble adjusting and we talked about it during spring training. I told him that he was trying to do too much too quickly, that it was going to take him one hundred games to get comfortable back at third base, where he had played when he first came up to the big leagues in '81 and '82. He'd been over at shortstop for a lot of years.

Consider the adjustments he had to make: His footwork had to be different, the throws he made were different, his responsibilities were different, and I could go on and on. That's why I told him it would take some time for him to acclimate to playing third again.

People say you can move from one position to another with no problem, but that's not really so. The Orioles were trying to tell Cal, "You'll have no trouble adjusting back to third base." That's not really true, because you've got to go out there on that field and take all these different type balls that you haven't been taking for fourteen or fifteen years. You've got to get your footwork together. You have to get your body together. That's why I told him point blank, "It's going to take you one hundred games to get comfortable back at third base."

The Orioles were trying to tell Cal, "You'll have no trouble adjusting back to third base." Well, that's not really true. That's why I told him point blank, "It's going to take you one hundred games to get comfortable."

Every position is a demanding position. Sure shortstop is demanding, but third base is demanding, too. Second base is demanding. First base is demanding. You can go out and take all the fungoes you want, but it's a different story when that game starts.

Look at a utility player. He plays third base today, second base tomorrow, shortstop the next day. He goes out there those three days in three different positions and has routine balls hit to him and he makes all the plays. Everybody says, "This guy will do a great job no matter where we put him." Then all of a sudden you take that same utility guy and you put him at third base for five days in a row. Now he doesn't make all those plays that he was making before, because he's getting different type balls hit to him.

> *Every position is a demanding position. Sure shortstop is demanding, but third base is demanding, too. You can go out and take all the fungoes you want, but it's a different story when that game starts.*

The same thing often happens with your fourth outfielder, your fill-in guy. You play him once in a while and when he's in there he fields the routine balls hit to him, maybe he gets a couple of hits, and he's done a great job. But when all of a sudden you have an injury to one of your regular outfielders and your fourth guy becomes an everyday player, the next thing you know he isn't making the plays. The ball's hit over his head in the alley. The ball's hit in front of him and he doesn't get in to make the play. He makes a throwing mistake. Quickly, you'll see the difference in that same ballplayer just because he became your everyday player. If there's one thing this game has taught me, it's that it takes time to adjust.

Cal didn't have any specific problems changing

positions, it was just the overall playing of the new position that he struggled with. For example, the ball might be hit hard, really scalded. Well, a shortstop has just a little bit longer to react to that ball. At third base, though, when it's hit hard you have a tendency to stiffen up on the ball, rather than playing it more softly. You have to experience that before you can adjust to it and do it.

Your footwork might be off just a little bit. You might be landing just a little bit late on your feet to get ready to make a play, and then as a result you're not able to move as quickly. As I say, it just takes time. I think when he heard me say that it was going to take one hundred games to adjust, he was satisfied and relieved, because he was trying to do it too quickly.

In three days a utility player might play three different positions, have routine balls hit to him, and make all the plays. Then that same guy plays third base five days in a row. Now he doesn't make all of those plays that he was making before, because he's getting different type balls hit to him.

ENDING THE CONSECUTIVE GAMES STREAK

On Sunday, September 20, 1998, the day that Cal decided to end his streak of 2,632 consecutive games played—ending what everyone regarded as one of the most remarkable feats in sports history—he called me a little after lunch to inform me of his decision to sit out the Orioles' final home game of the season that night.

It was the first time that we had ever discussed putting an end to the Streak. This may surprise some people, but the Streak was something we just didn't talk about. We didn't intentionally avoid the subject, it was just one of those things that never came up. The Streak wasn't something that was planned—it was simply the product of Cal's day-in, day-out commitment.

Anyway, when he called me that afternoon—his mother and I were both on the phone—I told him that I thought his decision to end it that night was a fine one. Simply put, I thought it was the right time to end it. I don't think it should have been done any sooner. If I had been looking at it from the other side, from a fan's perspective, I wouldn't have wanted him to end it then, but he had looked at it, and I understood what he was doing. I felt he was perfectly right in what he did, and he handled it all very, very well.

> *It was the first time that we had ever discussed putting an end to the Streak. I thought it was the right time to end it.*

Cal wasn't really asking us for an opinion. I know he had thought about this decision for a long time, which is what he does with every decision that he makes. And I very much agreed with it. Ultimately, he came to the conclusion that the Streak was a distraction, that it had become such a hassle that it was blurring the team's focus. I told him that it was wrong that people had made it into such a spectacle, but now that they had, it was probably time to get rid of it.

Cal wasn't really asking us for an opinion. I know he had thought about this decision for a long time, which is what he does with every decision that he makes. And I very much agreed with it.

The Streak is something that Cal should be immensely proud of. He surpassed Lou Gehrig's record string of consecutive games by 502—better than three full seasons. I can remember the first game of Cal's streak almost as vividly as his final game. It started on May 30, 1982. Cal batted eighth and played third base against Toronto. He played third base for the first twenty-seven games of the Streak, and when he ended it he was back at third base.

Ending the Streak took a burden off Cal's shoulders, but it also took a burden off of a lot of other people's shoulders. The organization didn't have to make a decision to stop the Streak or to get Cal out of the lineup. He did it for them. He accepted the responsibility of leadership and acted accordingly. This made life a lot easier for quite a few folks in the front office of the Orioles. He just lightened the load for them.

> *Ending the Streak took a burden off Cal's shoulders, but it also took a burden off of a lot of other people's shoulders. The organization didn't have to make a decision to stop the Streak, or to get Cal out of the lineup. He did it for them.*

LIFE AFTER THE STREAK

Now that the Streak is over, Cal, or his manager, may decide, "Okay, we just played a Saturday night game and the game went till 12:30 or one o'clock in the morning. We're coming back with a Sunday day game, and it might be a good idea to take this one off." That's the luxury that Cal gave his manager by ending the Streak.

Will Cal's record of 2,632 consecutive games ever be broken? Well, it's said that records are made to be broken, and someone might say, "Cal broke it, so if he can break it, somebody else can." My response is, I doubt it. The nature of the game today—with free agency, specialty players, and shorter careers—suggests to me that it won't happen. It's possible, but it would obviously take a very special player and a unique situation.

> *Will Cal's record ever be broken? Well, they say records are made to be broken, but my response is, I doubt it.*

In the game today, for example, you don't have guys coming to the big leagues at twenty and twenty-one years old, like a Jim Palmer, an Eddie Murray, or a Cal Ripken. We had a lot of guys who were in their early twenties coming to the big leagues through the Oriole system, and some other clubs did, too. Today you don't have that. You've got players coming into the big leagues who are twenty-five, twenty-six, and twenty-seven. Next thing you know, they've played ten years, they're thirty-seven or thirty-eight, and they're ready to retire.

You don't have people playing as long, or with the same club. It's rare today for someone to play sixteen or seventeen years in the big leagues at all, much less to play every game over that period. That alone will make it difficult for anyone to break Cal's record.

It's rare today for someone to play sixteen or seventeen years in the big leagues at all, much less to play every game over that period.

THE DEMANDS
OF STARDOM

Cal signs more autographs in a year than Babe Ruth and Lou Gehrig combined signed in their lifetimes. In the era that Ruth and Gehrig played, very few fans wanted an autograph. It was only the kids who sought the signatures of players. Today everybody is after autographs, because the memorabilia business has gotten so big in the last twenty years or so. You're talking about a multimillion-dollar industry.

Cal signs autographs before games, after games, and on his days off. He also receives in the neighborhood of ten thousand pieces of mail a month. It's gotten out of control.

In Ruth's day he could walk through Central Park and talk with the kids that were playing there. It was usually a manageable crowd. But that was a different era. If Ruth were playing today he'd have the same demands on him that Cal has. Ruth would come to the ballpark, and, like Cal does, get swamped by fans the second he stepped out of his car and started walking toward the clubhouse. Every time Cal comes to the ballpark, he has to get through at least five hundred people before he can even get into the clubhouse. He can't stand there and sign autographs for all five hundred people. He's got to get inside and get ready to go to work.

Cal signs more autographs in a year than Babe Ruth and Lou Gehrig combined signed in their lifetimes. He signs autographs before games, after games, and on his days off. He also receives in the neighborhood of ten thousand pieces of mail a month.

He always tries to sign as many autographs as he can, but he just can't please everyone. People get upset when Cal doesn't sign their ball or program, or if he gets taken into the ballpark through a separate gate, but they need to understand that he usually stands on the field or outside the park signing for an hour and a half after every ball game. Now, there are still some people out there after he's done signing, but he has to draw the line somewhere. Then when one person gets turned down, Cal's immediately a bad guy in their eyes because he wouldn't sign. The thing is, he can't please all of the people all of the time. But he still tries.

Every time Cal comes to the ballpark, he has to get through at least five hundred people before he can even get into the clubhouse. Obviously, he can't sign autographs for all five hundred people. He's got to get inside and get ready to go to work. The thing is, he can't please all of the people all of the time. But he still tries.

LEADERSHIP

What makes a leader? It's a seemingly simple question, but it's one that's very difficult to answer. In baseball, there are leaders who don't hit .350 or win twenty games. Then there are some guys who hit forty home runs and drive in 140 runs, and they aren't leaders. Really, what it comes down to is not an individual's production on the field—it comes down to the makeup of that individual.

A leader doesn't have to jump up and down. What one must do to become a leader is to gain the respect of the players on the club. One becomes a leader more as a result of the other people on the club making him a leader. A leader has to be a stand-up guy. He's got to be a guy who is himself, not somebody else.

One of the leaders on every club has to be the guy who has "manager" written over his door. When they put "manager" in front of his name, then he's the leader and he assumes the responsibilities of leadership. He shouldn't be looking for somebody else to take the responsibility of being a leader. I can't understand it when I hear a manager say something like, "We've got to have a leader on this club." What are you paying the manager for? If you need a leader, then fire the manager and get somebody else.

> *In baseball, there are leaders who don't hit .350 or win twenty games. Then there are some guys who hit forty home runs and drive in 140 runs, and they aren't leaders. A leader doesn't have to jump up and down. What one must do to become a leader on a team is to gain the respect of the players on the club.*

Though nobody gives him credit for it, Cal is by nature a leader. All you hear in the papers is, "Ownership wants Ripken to take a more vocal course in leadership of the club." That's not the way you lead. You lead by doing what you do every day. Cal has players come to him all the time asking him questions, and he answers them. And the player is a better player for the answer he got.

The thing is, Cal's a quiet person and he does everything in a quiet way. People want him to jump up and down, but they don't understand leadership. You don't have to scream and holler. Maybe once in a while you might say, "Come on guys, let's go, we're a little bit dead today." But you don't have to be raising hell, pointing fingers, and accusing people in the clubhouse. If it needs to be done, that's the manager's job, but if he's got any sense, the manager shouldn't be pointing fingers in meetings. He should be doing it privately, because if he's gotten that far, he's lost control of his ball club.

> *I can't understand it when I hear a manager say something like, "We've got to have a leader on this club." What are you paying the manager for? If you need a leader, then fire the manager and get somebody else.*

When I was coaching, I always tried to be a leader. I threw batting practice, I coached the bases, I helped the players. I talked to a player about a mistake. I didn't go around saying, "I'm a leader," but the things I did during the course of the day were all things that a leader does.

I didn't jump up and down and raise hell. On the bench I might have said, "Come on. Let's go here now.

We haven't gotten a damn base runner in three innings. It's time to get to this guy. Let's see if we can shake ourselves up a little bit." But I wasn't jamming it down somebody's throat when I was saying it. The players realize what has to be done. Sometimes they just need a little encouragement to get them going.

Cal has players come to him all the time asking him questions, and he answers them. And the player is a better player for the answer he got. Cal's a quiet person and he does everything in a quiet way.

MANAGER CAL JR.?

If he chooses to stay in baseball after he hangs up the spikes, Cal would make a very good manager, because he knows the game so well. He has a keen understanding of the intricacies and nuances of the game. Beyond that, he understands people. That's a big part of being a good manager: being able to understand and handle people.

> *Cal would make a very good manager, because he knows the game so well. Beyond that, he understands people. That's a big part of being a good manager.*

A lot of people say that it's difficult for a great player to manage because they have trouble being patient with players who aren't as talented as they were. Well, I don't think that'd be a problem for Cal, because he understands that part of the game. He knows how to deal with players who aren't as gifted as he is. What he wouldn't tolerate, however, are players who didn't give him 100 percent all the time.

Now, I can't really say if Cal will ever manage or not, because it's not something we've ever talked about. But as he's proved so many times in the past, Cal is capable of virtually anything.

Bill would also be a good coach, or a good manager, because he also understands the game, and he understands people. But I don't really think that he's given any thought to that part of the game at this particular time. You really don't think in those terms while you're playing.

> *Cal knows how to deal with players who aren't as gifted as he is. What he wouldn't tolerate, however, are players who didn't give him 100 percent all the time.*

CHAPTER 4

MANAGING AND COACHING

Do It Right

Practice doesn't make perfect, because you can practice bad habits and never get any better. Perfect practice is what makes perfect. You play like you practice, and if you practice correctly you'll play correctly.

GOOD PLAY IS
HABIT-FORMING

Everything that you do prior to the ball game should get you ready to play the game. The reason you practice is to form good habits on the sidelines, and then they become automatic in the game. That's why you take ground balls as an infielder. That's why you take fly balls as an outfielder. That's why you run the bases. That's why you take batting practice. So when the game starts, you'll do things the same way that you've done them in practice.

I've had kids in youth ball, and I've even had kids in the minor leagues, who have fooled around in practice and said, "Well, I wouldn't do that in the game," and I've said, "You're right, because you're not going to do it in my practice."

Mark Belanger started in baseball with me in the Northern League, in Aberdeen, South Dakota. He and Cal were both shortstops, and I was around both of them for many, many years. Not once did I ever see either of them go out and fool around while taking ground balls in batting practice. They may have caught the ball one-handed, but they caught the ball the correct way. So when the game came along, and that same ball was hit in the game, they just automatically went after the ball the same way, approached the ball the same way, caught the ball the same way, and made the throw the same way.

> *Everything that you do prior to the ball game should get you ready to play the game.*

That's why perfect practice makes perfect. You don't want to practice bad habits, you want to practice good habits. The only way to do something is to do it right. It doesn't take any longer to do something right than to do it halfway.

> *Perfect practice makes perfect. You don't want to practice bad habits, you want to practice good habits.*

LET THEM PLAY

Fundamentals are the best way to teach young players. If, for example, you're going out to sell insurance, you have to know what you're selling. The same applies to baseball. You have to know how to play in order to be a good player and enjoy the game.

To learn the game of baseball you have to go out and play it. As I tell the kids at my baseball school, I could hang up charts all the way around the gymnasium, and we could spend two weeks studying those charts, but they wouldn't realize the meaning of a lot of those things until they went out and played the game. You have to play to gain experience and you have to play to learn.

> ## *Fundamentals are the best way to teach young players.*

It's different at the major-league level. For example, in Baltimore, if the Orioles don't win they don't draw fans. Winning is the most important thing at the major-league level. But winning is not the most important thing at the Little League level. I know Little League people get upset with me for making that statement.

> *To learn the game of baseball you have to go out and play it. You have to play to gain experience and you have to play to learn.*

At the baseball school, we have the kids for one week. We work those kids very hard in that week, because they're coming there to learn—that's why people are sending their kids to school. But in the evenings, we play ball games. I want those games played because I want the kids to have fun, and you have to play in order to learn.

> *Winning is the most important thing at the major-league level. But winning is not the most important thing at the Little League level.*

KIDS TODAY

I think we can safely say that we live in a computer world. Kids today sit down, turn on those computers, televisions, and tape players, and their fingers are flying. Well, I'm too dumb to do that. But today's kids just push the buttons and make things happen.

Kids are more susceptible to knowledge today than we were years ago. Television is one of the reasons for that. It was pretty tough to see what was happening on that radio. I believe that at an early age, today's kids are much smarter than we were years ago. So I'm not opposed to kids having instruction. But it should start with the fundamentals, and there should be an element of fun to it.

I'm not opposed to kids having instruction. But it should start with the fundamentals, and there should be an element of fun to it.

HOW TO IMPROVE YOUR LITTLE LEAGUE PRACTICE

I say this to Little League coaches time after time: Take your team out in the field to practice. You should have assistant coaches. If you don't have enough assistants, there are going to be enough parents sitting in the stands during practice who all know how things should be done, and they'll be quick to tell you how to do things if they don't think you're doing them right. I suggest you use those parents.

Utilize more people and have a number of things going on at one time in the practices. Don't have the practices last three hours. Also make sure a coach throws some batting practice, and make sure every player gets to hit the ball in batting practice.

My message to coaches of young players is that by having shorter practices and doing more things at one time, you keep the attention of your kids. After a while kids lose concentration, particularly when they're standing around doing nothing for a long period of time.

My message to coaches of young players is that by having shorter practices and doing more things at one time, you keep the attention of your kids.

Don't over-instruct, but have fun, and make the game fun. Make those kids want to come back for practice the next day, or two days from now. Have those kids wanting to come to the ballpark for the game. I know it's a difficult thing, but at that age level—and even when they get to high school—the most important thing is that they're having fun at what they're doing. It's a game and they need to enjoy it. But they also need to work at it.

Make those kids want to come back for practice the next day. Have those kids wanting to come to the ballpark for the game.

THE GREATEST FUN
IN BASEBALL

This has taken place a lot in Little League and in other youth leagues: A little guy comes out to practice, he's the smallest guy on the team, and the coach says, "Okay, we're gonna get five swings." Well, in five swings this little fellow never makes contact with the ball. Then the coach tells him, "Run to first base." Then the game starts and that little guy goes up to home plate, and the coach says, "Don't take the bat off your shoulder, and you'll walk." Well, the greatest fun in the game of baseball is hitting a baseball, and every player should have a chance to do it.

The greatest fun in the game of baseball is hitting a baseball, and every player should have a chance to do it.

IT'S STILL JUST A GAME

The only things I ever showed Cal and Billy when they were small was how to catch a fly ball and how to catch a ground ball. Then when they got older, and they were in high school, I had a batting cage out in the backyard, where I would work with them more extensively in the fundamentals of the game. They got a lot of instruction, although I didn't over-instruct.

My daughter Ellen was also well-schooled in the fundamentals of softball. Quite early on she picked up the right way to throw, for example. Then she continued to practice good habits, so they became automatic, and she was able to apply the fundamentals. That's what you have to do.

The kids and I talked about things and we did things physically, as far as instruction and fundamentals were concerned, but when they were small I didn't believe in going out and working on fundamentals and drills to the extent that a lot of people do today.

It's still a game, and a game should be fun. I used those words when I was in baseball, I use those words at my baseball school, and I still use those words today when I talk about major-league ballplayers.

When people talk about major-league players today, the first thing they want to talk about is salary. It so happens that they make a lot of money, but I talk about major-league players playing the game because they love to play the game of baseball.

Major league players make a lot of money, but they play the game because they love to play the game of baseball.

THE FIELD AS A
CLASSROOM

I've done a great deal of teaching in my life in baseball, both in the minor leagues and in the big leagues. I never looked at it with an overflowing abundance of satisfaction when a guy picked up something, or when I was able to help him, because I felt that I could help anybody, I could improve anybody. It was just a matter of getting the opportunity to work with them.

Sure, you're satisfied, you're pleased, but I didn't get overjoyed when this guy went out and did something successfully because of what I was able to help him with. I felt that that was part of my job, and that it was just a natural thing. I guess after you're away from it and out of it, then you really get more satisfaction, and you're a little bit happier about it than you were at the time.

I was always happy that I was helping someone, but that's just my nature. I've always wanted to help players. If I can help you, you're going to be a better player.

If you're a better player, we're a better team. If we're a better team, I'm a better manager.

If I can help you, you're going to be a better player. If you're a better player, we're a better team. If we're a better team, I'm a better manager.

It's different at my baseball school, where I'm working with much younger players. I get instant satisfaction over there. I can be working with a young guy and five minutes later see so much improvement. There's great satisfaction in working with the young kids there.

With young players, in some areas, they're not going to see improvement right away. They might not see it for three or four years down the road. In fact, as I tell the players at the baseball school, some of the things that they learn here, they may not apply for three or four years. But then that situation will come up and they'll do it automatically, and they'll say, "Oh, I remember when we learned that." Everything just doesn't come up every day in baseball, or in life.

> *With young players, in some areas, they're not going to see improvement right away. They might not see it for three or four years down the road. Because everything just doesn't come up every day in baseball, or in life.*

HOW MUCH COACHING IS ENOUGH?

Some players need less coaching than others. How do you tell when that's the case with a particular player? You don't have to tell—they'll tell you. You'll know just by watching them. It'll be quickly apparent.

That's the case if you can tell a guy something one time. Maybe he'll walk away from you, and you don't know whether he's agreed with what you said or not or whether he's going to go try it. The next thing you know, you're looking at how he's adapted what you've told him to his style or to his ability, and he's executing that particular fundamental to the top notch. And you haven't said anything else to him.

With other players, you have to work a little harder to convince them. There are some players whom you don't convince. Those are the ones who fall by the wayside.

Jim Palmer was a guy who didn't need a lot of coaching in the minor leagues. Evidently, he had had a good coach around him prior to his coming into professional baseball. That, along with his interest in the game—he studied each game from the time the game started until it was over—made him an extremely intelligent and successful player. You could show him something one time and that's all you had to do. He just went out and did it. Tell him once and that was it, he'd put it to use.

We had a lot of players like that in our system over the years. Generally speaking, that type of individual is going to be a better player. If not excellent players, they're at least going to be good players. They're able to recognize what needs to be done and how to go about doing it. They can make the necessary adjustments, and they can make the readjustments.

Some players need less coaching than others. They're able to recognize what needs to be done and how to go about doing it. With other players, you have to work a little harder to convince them. There are some players whom you don't convince. Those are the ones who fall by the wayside.

THE IMPORTANCE
OF FUNDAMENTALS

During my years in the Baltimore organization, fundamentals were always emphasized greatly. They're the basics of the game. That was always the strength of the Oriole ball clubs: They didn't make mistakes—the other team made the mistakes.

That was a big part of the success of the Orioles for years. We had good talent, but we had good, basic fundamentals. At the major-league level, the fundamentals were stressed in spring training, and we worked on them and executed them.

Fundamentals are the basics of the game. That was always the strength of the Oriole ball clubs: They didn't make mistakes—the other team made the mistakes.

There's still an emphasis on fundamentals today, but I'm not sure that they're taught the correct way and worked on enough. Yes, there are still clubs that stress fundamentals. But the name of the game is pitching, defense, and offense. If you've got good pitching and you've got good defense, then you don't have to score nine hundred runs to win. If you make the plays defensively by basic fundamentals of fielding, and you pitch with the basic fundamentals of pitching, and you use your bunt plays and you execute the fundamentals of offense, then you're going to be a successful club.

If you've got good pitching and you've got good defense, then you don't have to score nine hundred runs to win.

WHAT MAKES A
GOOD MANAGER

To be a good manager in any league, the first thing you've got to be able to do is handle people. You have to have command of your ball club and your players have to have confidence in you, because you've shown them that you know how to go about the game. Then you've got to go out and teach the fundamentals of the game and get your players to execute those fundamentals.

When you show your players that you know how to play the game, how the game should be played, and the correct fundamentals, you earn their confidence. Not only do you instruct—"This is how we do it"—but you also explain—"This is *why* we do it this way. This is the best way to do it." Proving your point allows you to have that command. You have to know how to handle people—not only as players, but as individuals. It all works hand in hand.

Everybody becomes a better player as a result of learning the fundamentals. Then you just keep adding on to all of that. You have to make the right moves at the right time, you have to do certain things, but those types of things all fall in line. They dictate themselves.

> *To be a good manager, the first thing you've got to be able to do is handle people. If you handle your people correctly, you'll get the most out of them.*

Naturally, you have to have talent on your club to be a successful manager. I always felt that I could run a ball club, but one thing I've always said is "If you want to be a good manager, have good players." That's the best way to be a good manager. I was always blessed with good talent in the minor leagues.

> *You want to have good talent, but also remember that the individual who's not the .300 hitter or the thirty-home-run hitter can still be a good talent, too, because he can do so many little things to help your club.*

I had very good talent on my '64 club at Class C Aberdeen, South Dakota. We had seven future major leaguers on that club—pitchers Jim Palmer, Eddie Watt, and Dave Leonhard, outfielder Lou Piniella, shortstop Mark Belanger, catcher Andy Etchebarren, and first baseman Mike Fiore—and we went 81-34, won the pennant by twelve games, and I was named Northern League Manager of the Year.

It takes everyone on a ball club to make it a successful team.

But there are a lot of players who aren't blessed with the talent to hit .300 or thirty home runs who can still do things to help your club offensively, by moving runners along on the bases, bunting a ball, and playing their defensive positions well. You want to have good talent, but also remember that the individual who's not the .300 hitter or the thirty-home-run hitter can still be a good talent, too, because he can do so many little things to help your club.

Sure, it's nice to have the twenty-five-game winner and the thirty-home-run hitter, but you can look at some of the clubs that are winning in the major leagues today, such as the New York Yankees, and see that it takes a combination of everyone on that ball club to make it a successful team.

Your manager has got to win you ten or twelve ball games a year with what he does. But mostly the players on the field are the ones who are going to win games. If they go out and execute the fundamentals and perform, you'll be fine. Earlier I said, if you want to be a good manager, get good players, but in getting good players, the manager still has to handle those people, and that becomes an important part of his job. That's why I list that as the most important quality for a manager.

If you handle your people correctly, you'll get the most out of them. Everybody's an individual. You have club rules, but you have to handle each individual as an individual. That's not to be confused with having a "club rule" and an "individual rule"—that's an entirely different issue. You have your club rules, and everybody adheres to those rules, but the manager also has to handle people in an individual way, by talking to each player and getting the most out of each one. You might have to kick one guy in the tail a little bit, you might have to pat one guy on the back—you might have to do both sometimes, but as long as the player knows what you're doing, why you're doing it, and how you're doing it, then you won't have any problems.

A manager has to handle people in an individual way, by talking to each player and getting the most out of each individual. You might have to kick one guy in the tail a little bit, you might have to pat one guy on the back—you might have to do both sometimes.

I know I never had any problems with any ball-players. I think every player who ever played for me respected me very much, and I think I earned that respect. I've never said anything to a player to hurt him. Anything I've ever said to any player was always to help him. Respect is a two-way street. The players have to be respected, too, and I was always aware of that.

Respect is a two-way street. The players have to be respected, too.

ABOVE: *Displaying my sliding technique in a 1957 game with the Phoenix Stars of the Arizona-Mexico League.*

RIGHT: *That's me, with the 1958 Wilson Tob's of the Carolina League.*

BELOW: *Trying to put the tag on a runner at the plate in a 1961 game for Double A Little Rock.*

RIGHT AND BELOW: Four-year-old Elly gives two-and-a-half-year-old Cal some pointers on his windup.

BELOW: Billy, Elly, and Cal (already wearing the Oriole uniform) have Fred pretty well buried in the sand at Daytona Beach in the spring of 1969.

TOP: *Cal (middle row, center) with his Little League team, the Aberdeen Indians, in 1970.*

ABOVE: *Elly takes a cut in a 1983 softball game.*

LEFT: *Cal in action with the Triple A Rochester Red Wings in 1981.*

LEFT: *Hitting a grounder to Cal during infield practice in spring training.*

BELOW: *Making a point in a spring training bunting drill with Kiko Garcia (3) and Gary Roenicke (35).*

BOTTOM: *Bill, Cal, and me in 1987, my first year as Orioles manager, and Bill's first in the big leagues.*

Throwing batting practice in '87.

Cal and me.

Plotting strategy on the mound in '87.

©Jerry Wachter Photography

Cal and Bill in Camden Yards in 1993, Bill's first year with Texas.

©The Tufton Group

ABOVE: Cal at the plate on September 6, 1995, the night he broke Lou Gehrig's record for consecutive games played.

RIGHT: Cal acknowledging the Camden Yards crowd on his record-setting night.

Richard F. Lasner

Richard F. Lasner

CLASS
ABILITY
LONGEVITY

With Vi alongside, I served as honorary grand marshal in a 1992 parade celebrating Aberdeen's centennial.

FROM THE MINORS
TO THE MAJORS

I managed the same way throughout baseball, from the minor leagues to the big leagues. The only thing I did differently at the minor-league level was stay with my starting pitcher longer.

For example, say I have a John Montague and a Bill Kirkpatrick, two young starters who pitched for me at Triple A Rochester, both of whom had pitched the previous year in Class A ball. At the Triple A level I'd give those two young pitchers the opportunity to get out of a tough jam, maybe in the fifth or sixth inning of a ball game, whereas in the major leagues I might go to my bullpen earlier. At Triple A I was trying to develop two pitchers to go on and be nine-inning pitchers at the major-league level.

I also had to be more patient with minor-league starting pitchers out of necessity. Today, pretty much all minor-league clubs have twenty-five-man rosters—that's in Class A, Double A, and Triple A—whereas years ago B clubs, in the low minors, might carry seventeen players, and at one time they carried only six-teen. Triple A clubs at that time had twenty-one-man rosters. In those days starters went out to pitch nine innings, not just five or six. In the lower minor leagues you let that pitcher go. He might get in trouble, but as long as he had his good stuff, you continued to let him stay out on the mound and work out that problem. You did that all the way through the minor leagues, because you were gearing pitchers to pitch nine innings. That's not happening as much today, which is one reason why you see fewer complete games pitched in the major leagues.

As far as managing the ball game—the bunt, the hit-and-run, the steal, all of those things—it's the same in the major leagues and the minor leagues. The game is played the same way.

> *Pitchers used to be geared in the minor leagues to pitch nine innings. But that's not happening as much today, which is one reason why you see fewer complete games pitched in the major leagues.*

THE PERILS
OF OVERMANAGING

Baseball is a simple game, but I think there are a lot of people who make it more difficult than it really is. For example, there are managers who try to complicate the game, but they've really got to just let those players do the playing. Sometimes managers want to overmanage, instead of just letting their players go out and play the game.

Many of today's managers are trying to do too much, and make too many moves. For example, take the lefty-righty thing today. There are some lefthanders in the bullpen who are going to come in and get that lefthanded hitter out. But there are also some lefthanded hitters who are going to hit that lefthander out of the ballpark. What I mean is that there are some righthanders who can come in and get a lefthanded hitter out as well as— or better than—a lefthander can. I think sometimes the manager takes away from the righthander's ability to do his job when he brings the lefthander in to do the job that the righthander could have done himself.

Sometimes managers want to overmanage, instead of just letting their players go out and play the game.

I just think there's too much emphasis placed on lefty-righty matchups today. You're not going to take Bert Blyleven and Nolan Ryan and Roger Clemens and those type of pitchers out of a game for that reason, yet you'll take another guy out. Sure, maybe the other pitcher is of a lesser quality, but still in all he's good. He's capable of getting a guy out. I think sometimes you have to let him do that.

There's too much specialization in baseball today. It used to be that if you were in the bullpen, you were a reliever, and if you were a starter, you were a starter. Now, today, everybody wants those jobs categorized and labeled: spot starters, long relievers, middle relievers, short relievers, righthanded setup men, left-handed setup men, closers. You can't always do that. The makeup of your club dictates what you can do and what you can't do.

Utilize the strength of your people and try to take advantage of the weaknesses of the other team's people.

Today it seems a manager always has to start the ninth inning with his closer. If he's got that type of closer, fine, but that closer doesn't always have his best stuff. If the manager doesn't bring in that closer, though, and things go wrong, then it's the manager's fault. Well, the manager's not going to put himself on the spot. He's going to bring that closer in every time.

But two or three days down the road you might be a better, stronger club if the guy who started the game had pitched the eighth and ninth innings, or if the reliever who pitched the eighth inning had pitched the ninth. It's all in the way ball clubs are built today, though, in comparison to how they were built years ago. It's the makeup of the clubs.

There are also too many stats today. Say the manager has a lefthanded hitter at home plate, a good lefthander, but the opposing manager brings in a lefthanded pitcher. So he goes to the bench, and he brings a righthanded pinch-hitter off the bench, because that's what the statistics dictate that he does. Sometimes that righthander he's bringing off the bench is a whole lot lesser hitter than the one he just pinch-hit for. The manager is going to go by the book, though. If he makes that move and it doesn't work, there's an automatic defense mechanism. He can say, "I did it according to the book." If the manager takes a chance and it blows up, then he's at risk. Well, I don't think there's any book to managing a ball club. You utilize the strengths of your people and you try to take advantage of the weaknesses of the other team's people. As long as you can put yourself in a position to do that, then you're doing your job as a manager. The stats don't necessarily have to support your decision.

Phil Rizzuto once recalled how Casey Stengel, the great Yankees manager, would study his players' faces before choosing a pinch hitter. "He could look into your eyes and see if you were going to get a base hit," Rizzuto said. Those are called gut decisions, and you don't see a lot of those made today. Instead, it all comes down to playing the percentages: What's this guy hitting against this particular pitcher?

It's okay if you send someone up to hit because you've got a gut feeling that he's going to go up to home plate and drive a runner in. Or he's going to get on base. Or he's going to do something to get this run in. A gut feeling is an entirely different thing from a hunch, though. Sometimes I hear people say, "I played a hunch." Well, I don't believe in hunches. Hunches are kind of like hope, and hope isn't worth a damn. Facts are better.

Hope isn't worth a damn. Facts are better.

Gut feelings are fine, but you still want to utilize your strengths. Sure, you're going to get the hell beaten out of you in some games. But you don't worry about those. You come back tomorrow, and it's 0–0. And I can give you all the scores of next year's American League games, because they never change—they're the same scores every year. Sometimes they're 18–1, sometimes they're 1–0. 2–1, 4–2, 3–2, all those same numbers are going to come up, year in and year out.

Sure, you're going to get the hell beaten out of you in some games. But you don't worry about those. You come back tomorrow, and it's 0–0.

THE TOPIC
OF TEMPERAMENT

The type of temperament that a manager has doesn't matter—what matters is that the manager has to be himself. He can't be two different people. If he's a soft-spoken guy, he should be soft-spoken. If he's a fiery guy, he's got to be a fiery guy. But he's also got to let his people know what his demeanor is, and that because he's quiet or fiery doesn't mean he's not going to be a good manager. He's got to be himself, but he's got to have his people understand him. That's very important.

You can win with any sort of temperament. Joe Torre won the World Series with the Yankees last year, and he had a pretty mellow, soft-spoken demeanor— perfectly suited for his personality and the ball club's. I also remember Earl Weaver winning the World Series, and you're not going to get any fierier than Earl. When you were losing, Earl wasn't fiery, Earl was sympathetic. But when you were winning, boy, he was fiery.

People understood, though. Earl didn't change, the players didn't change, but the players had to understand Earl. Earl had to understand the players, and he did. The manager of a ball club is the guy who is respected and who commands that respect. It's not up to the manager to adjust to his people. His people have to, and should, respect the manager.

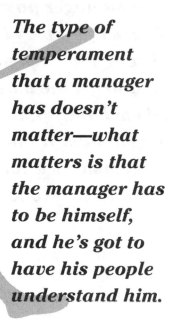

The type of temperament that a manager has doesn't matter—what matters is that the manager has to be himself, and he's got to have his people understand him.

The manager still has to figure out a way to get through to each player, though, and to get the most out of each player. There have been managers who got themselves in trouble because, in my estimation, they didn't use good, sound judgment—they didn't judge their people accurately and find a way to work with each person's temperament. You can't change the individual. Sometimes you'll hear people say that temperaments clashed. Well, what that means is that there was a lack of communication, and as a manager you can't afford a lot of that. You've got to have a line of communication open to everyone. The manager has to communicate, and the players have to communicate.

> *The manager has to figure out a way to get through to each player and to get the most out of each player. He has to have a line of communication open to everyone.*

DEALING WITH MISTAKES

Physical mistakes are part of the game. They've been happening for 130 years, and they'll be happening for 130 more. Mental mistakes can be corrected, just as physical mistakes can be corrected. As a manager, though, I waited until the next day to talk to a player about either type of mistake.

The player himself knows more than anybody else that he made a mistake. If you don't make mistakes, you're not going to learn anything. They're part of the game.

In the minor leagues I never worried about the number of physical errors a player made. The only thing I judged a player in the minor leagues on was his hands—his ability with the glove—not the number of errors he made. That's because the playing surfaces in the minor leagues aren't always good. They're not always good in the big leagues, either.

Mark Belanger made a slew of errors for me as a shortstop in Class A ball, in the Northern League, but the playing surfaces were terrible. So when I graded Mark Belanger's defensive abilities, I graded them as excellent. I knew that on a better field he wouldn't have made that many errors.

As a manager in the minor and major leagues, I was very patient with errors. If a player continued to make physical mistakes and mental errors, however, then it was time to find somebody who wasn't going to make those mistakes.

> *The player himself knows more than anybody else that he made a mistake. If you don't make mistakes, you're not going to learn anything. They're part of the game.*

Some people believe that you should be less tolerant of mental mistakes than physical mistakes. I disagree, because mental mistakes are going to be made, too. The way the human body and the nervous system operate, those things are going to happen. That's part of the game. I don't care who the player is— somewhere, sometime, he's going to make a bad mental mistake. But it won't happen again, because the player will benefit from that mental mistake. The club that makes the fewest physical and mental errors is the club that's going to win, because the other team's going to lose.

Sometimes when a young player in the big leagues

makes a mistake, they'll say it was a "rookie mistake," but often it was a fundamental mistake, and that
shouldn't be happening. Although that player may be
new to the big leagues, he's been playing baseball his
whole life, and it's still the same game, regardless of
what level you're playing at. That goes back to the fundamentals being taught properly in the minor leagues.
The player who has had those lessons is far less prone
to those sorts of errors in the big leagues.

> *The club that makes*
> *the fewest physical*
> *and mental errors is*
> *the club that's going*
> *to win.*

With free agency today, a player isn't coming through
one farm system, and often a player isn't playing a long
time in the minors like they did years ago. The abilities
of some organizations to teach the fundamentals could
be limited. Maybe there's not enough stress put on fundamentals. I believe that's why, in today's game of baseball, it's more important than ever for an organization to develop its own players to move up to the big
leagues. That provides more opportunity to stress the
fundamentals. The salary structure will almost certainly be more manageable. The clubhouse chemistry
will automatically be better. My feeling toward major-

league clubs today is that they'd better stop worrying about the clubhouse chemistry, and start worrying about getting a guy out. That's a whole lot more important than chemistry.

Major-league clubs had better stop worrying about the clubhouse chemistry, and start worrying about getting a guy out.

A MATTER OF STYLE

Sometimes you'll hear people say that certain fundamentals, such as the bunt, are lost arts in baseball today. I don't think they're lost, it's just a matter of the type of ball club that you have. The bunt is not really a lost art, but the defense of the bunt is so good today that it has become harder to execute it.

Also, look at the makeup of most big-league clubs today: They didn't used to have a big guy playing second base and a big guy playing centerfield like most clubs do nowadays. Today they're talking about power, rather than hit-and-runs, one-at-a-time runs, and that sort of thing. It's a different game.

From that side of it, the bunt isn't a lost art, it's just not used as often. It's still used and it's still executed, but it's not executed as much as it used to be, because there were more players who really worked at bunting and getting a man over to the next base and then driving that run in.

But that was in a period when the earned run averages for pitching staffs were in the 2.00s and 3.00s. Today, the Atlanta Braves and maybe a few other clubs are the only teams with an earned run average for their staff that's under 4.00. Teams are giving up entirely too many runs. When they give up more, they've got to score more. It's a vicious circle. It's a different style of baseball.

A major-league club has to go out at the beginning of the season with the idea of scoring at least eight hundred runs— that's an average of five runs per game. If they do that they can win a hundred ball games.

It's really difficult for a team today to win with pitching and by manufacturing runs. Atlanta could come close with its pitching staff, and there are a couple of other clubs that put up good numbers with their pitching staffs, but they still have to score five runs a game to win. They're going to win some games 3–2, 2–1, and 3–1. They can do that if they have a good pitching staff, but they're still going to have some 9–8 games.

A major-league club has to go out at the beginning of the season with the idea of scoring at least eight hundred runs—that's an average of five runs per game. If they do that they can win a hundred ball games. Of the eight teams that made the playoffs in 1998, the San

Diego Padres were the only one that failed to score at least five runs a game and finish in the top ten in the big leagues in runs scored.

When they get to the postseason, it's a different story. Each team has its three top pitchers starting in the playoffs. They don't figure to score as many runs, so they might be more inclined to play for one run and use the sacrifice bunt. Still, they have to use what got them there in the first place. There again, they have to take advantage of their players' strengths—and not expose their weaknesses—at home plate, or defensively, or whatever. They shouldn't be bunting with a hitter who can't execute the bunt.

> *When they get to the postseason, it's a different story. Still, they have to use what got them there in the first place. They shouldn't be bunting with a hitter who can't execute the bunt.*

People say, "Anybody in the major leagues ought to be able to bunt a ball." Well, bunting isn't that easy. It's easy if you're very deliberate and go about it correctly, but if you don't, bunting is very difficult. It's a whole lot different going out and bunting a ball off of the coach or the guy on your own team's staff who's throwing batting practice than it is against a guy who's throwing a ninety-seven-mile-an-hour fastball. You have to go about it like anything else: If you're going to be successful at it, you've got to go out and work at it, and you've got to practice it correctly in order to be able to do it automatically in a game.

I don't recall Earl Weaver ever putting a bunt on with someone at the plate who wasn't capable of getting the bunt down. He would bring on somebody to pinch hit who was more capable, if that's what he wanted to do. He always utilized the strengths of his players, and that's what you have to do.

People say, "Anybody in the major leagues ought to be able to bunt a ball." Well, bunting isn't that easy.

CHAPTER 5

OUTSIDE THE LINES

The Oriole Way

Having your club follow certain rules, and having players come through your system on their way to the major leagues respecting those rules—that was the Baltimore way, the Oriole way, and people in the organization were proud of that. They were proud to be Orioles.

A WINNING
ORGANIZATION

I was fortunate, of course, to have been in the Baltimore organization for all those years, and in those days the Orioles had strict organizational rules. As I moved from the bottom of the ladder to the top, I had the opportunity to see many of the organization's top players at some level. No matter the level, though, those rules were always respected and upheld by all the people in authority in the organization. No one took issue with those club rules because everybody respected them. As you moved along in the organization as a player, manager, or coach, and when you got to the big leagues, it was the same thing. Those rules were real, and you knew what they were. You knew what to expect and you respected that. That made it easy, not only for the player, but also for the manager and the coach.

Brooks Robinson, Bobby Grich, Mark Belanger, Jim Palmer, Dave Leonhard, Eddie Watt, Dennis Martinez, Rich Dauer, Eddie Murray, Mike Flanagan, Al Bumbry, Don Baylor. I can keep on naming them and naming them. Those guys all came through the Oriole system and went to the big leagues, and that's one of the reasons they were such solid players, other than, of course, the talent they possessed. Having players come through that system and knowing the way things operate, how they operate, and why they operate—that was the key to the Orioles' success.

That's not to say that the Orioles were the only team to have that kind of system. There were other organizations that were good organizations and good systems. I speak of the Orioles because that was the system I was involved with. If major-league organizations today were able to develop their own talent and bring it through their farm systems the way we did, they'd be better off all the way around.

> *Having players come through the system and knowing the way things operate, how they operate, and why they operate—that was the key to the Orioles' success.*

Generally speaking, coaches and managers still have to teach in the major leagues today, as they do in every level of baseball. But years ago, in the Baltimore organization, there wasn't the need for a whole lot of teaching at the major-league level, because most of the players had come through the system, from D to C to B to A to Double A to Triple A to the big leagues. Everything was done from the major-league level down to the lowest minor-league club in exactly the same way. Those players in the minor leagues already knew how to play the game when they got to the big leagues. They weren't coming from another system that did things a different way. They did things the way the Baltimore Orioles did things.

For example, at the A level the pickoff play was the same as it was in the big leagues. The bunt plays were the same. The rundown plays. The cutoffs. The relays. All of those things were done the same way at D, C, B, A, Double A, Triple A, and the major leagues. For whichever position you played, you knew: This is where you had to be on this particular play. By the time a player got to the big leagues, it was just automatic.

I've always been someone who was big on rules and discipline. When Edward Bennett Williams, who was then the owner, made me the Orioles manager before the '87 season, he recalled a trip to Japan in '84 during which I didn't loosen my tie for the entire seventeen-hour flight. That's a true story, but he apparently didn't take that into consideration in 1988, six games into the season, when he fired me.

No, I didn't loosen the tie, and we were always a coat-and-tie organization. The first time that policy was relaxed was when Earl Weaver said that no tie was required on charter flights. That was fine, although I would've preferred it if he had left it alone, because it didn't make any difference to me whether it was a charter flight or not. I always wore a coat and tie.

Once when we were in New York on a road trip my hotel room was broken into, and my wallet and money were stolen. I went down to the front desk, because I needed to get a check cashed. They sent me to the appropriate person, and the woman asked me how I could be identified. I said, "The only thing I can do is get you to call Earl Weaver and tell him what my problem is."

If major-league organizations today were able to develop their own talent and bring it through their farm systems the way the Orioles did, they'd be better off all the way around.

She did, and the first thing Earl asked her was, "Does he have a coat and tie on?" She said, "No, he doesn't have a tie on."—I had a coat on, but I had been in a hurry to get down there and hadn't put a tie on. So I said to her, "Tell Earl that I just came from my room down to your office." He heard me on the phone, and he said, "That's him, because I know that voice." So everything worked out, but I was always known for wearing that coat and tie.

We were a proud organization, we were a good organization, and those rules were part of our makeup. I always wore the coat and tie, no matter what, and I think those are things that are club policy and you keep them club policy. They've since been relaxed, I know, but I wouldn't have been the one to relax them.

BUILDING A CHAMPION

To me, the best way to build a good club is to develop players in your farm system. If you can't do that at a particular position, you need to get the talent elsewhere. Today, at the major-league level, the free-agent market is the place. Although the best talent is always going to be high-priced.

People may say, "What about the '98 Yankees? They brought in a lot of players from the outside and won a championship. How do you explain their success?" Well, number one, they've got good talent: They've got good pitching, they've got good defense, and they can swing the bat. That's one reason they're where they are. Joe Torre is another reason—his handling of that ball club. That goes back to the importance of handling people as well as managing a ball club.

In a way, one might say the Yankees bought a pennant—they had the second-highest payroll in the big leagues in 1998—but I don't think that going out and purchasing a high-priced player means that you're buying a pennant.

You have to have some continuity on a winning ball

club, and you have to have a foundation to build on. The Yankees have that. They have a core of guys who have come up through their system: Bernie Williams, Derek Jeter, Mariano Rivera, Andy Pettitte, Jorge Posada, Ramiro Mendoza, Ricky Ledee. They added to that core through trades and free agency, but they were also careful about the players they acquired—they brought in people who would fit.

Years ago owner Gene Autry brought in a lot of high-priced talent to the California Angels. The Yankees themselves tried bringing in a lot of free agents in the '80s. It didn't work in either case, because there wasn't enough continuity, there wasn't enough of a core of talent, and the players didn't fit together to form a cohesive ball club.

> *The best way to build a good club is to develop players in your farm system, but that takes devotion by the ownership and the organization to put some money into it.*

The game has changed because of free agency. With the Oriole clubs in the '60s and '70s, we sat down at the end of the year and decided what our needs were—who were the players we had that we wanted to keep. Then we went ahead and signed those players. But the focus was on our own people.

Today with free agency, the front offices all are talking about the big money and the free-agent players, and they don't worry about the lesser player who does a good job for the club. The poor guy who's not in the free-agent market and isn't out there commanding that kind of money is handicapped. They don't have to worry about signing him or doing anything with him right away. He's going to be there after everything else is all done.

An awful lot of the big free agents are making a lot of money. That doesn't mean guys are money-hungry. The owners have put the money out there. I don't think you should evaluate players by how much money they make. For example, David Cone makes a lot of money, but he performs well—he won twenty games last year. Money shouldn't enter into it.

> *An awful lot of the big free agents are making a lot of money. That doesn't mean guys are money-hungry. The owners have put the money out there.*

It's possible to win today by developing your own players, but it would take some time and good fortune to do it. Montreal, for example, hasn't gotten away from developing its own people. Unfortunately, for the Expos the money issue enters into it.

Basically, they've put a representative team on the field by bringing up people from their farm system and developing their own prospects. They didn't go out and buy up free agents. Sure, they've gotten some talent back in getting rid of their better players, the guys who were evidently going to put them over the hump salary-wise. But I don't understand why the ownership of that club doesn't hold on to those players and try to put as good a club out on the field as they can. That's where I don't understand ownership.

I know that there are financial issues for these so-called small-market teams, but I still think that if a major-league club puts a representative team on the field, they'll draw the crowds. I know it's a changed game with new stadiums and a different flow of people coming to the park, and yes, baseball is more of an entertainment industry today, but I still feel that to draw and to be successful you've got to put a good team on the field. Everything else will take care of itself.

But a team with better resources should definitely be able to build through its farm system. The Orioles can do it. The Dodgers can do it; they've brought a lot of guys up through their system, which is evidently still pretty good. The Yankees still have some good talent down on the farm. It takes devotion by ownership and the organization to put some money into the team and go about developing players that way. With free agency today and ownership geared toward the quick-fix, I'm not sure that owners or players would want to get back to developing a farm system and developing their own people, but it can be done. If this was done it would be a whole lot less of a burden for teams in terms of salaries.

I can't see it really taking place in the near future, though, because that guy whose club finished third last year is going to go out and get a couple of free agents to try and finish first this year. He's not going to bring a guy out of the farm system.

CHEMISTRY

For years, when the Orioles were promoting players from within, all of those guys had come up through the organization, so they knew the rules when they got to the big leagues. That was the chemistry—the chemistry was already there. You didn't have to do anything to alter the chemistry, you just went out and continued to play baseball and do the job.

When you brought one guy in as a free agent, the twenty-four other guys on the major-league club made that one guy an Oriole. He had come to Rome, and he had no choice but to do as the Romans did, or they'd run him out of town. Today, it's the other way around. You've got one or two guys on your club who are Orioles, or Astros, or Padres, or whatever, so you don't have that same chemistry. You're not going to have it, so you've got to do things well all the way around to compensate for the lack of it.

Chemistry is great, but chemistry doesn't get any hits or get anybody out. You have to have the right type of people and they have to be able to perform. If they don't perform and you don't win, where's your chemistry? You don't have any. But if you perform and you win, you have chemistry.

When Baltimore brought one guy in as a free agent, the twenty-four other guys on the club made that one guy an Oriole. He had come to Rome, and he had no choice but to do as the Romans did.

Pride has a lot to do with producing good chemistry. Take the Yankees. What's the first word that goes behind the Yankees? Yankee pride. Well, the Orioles always had Oriole pride. "It's great to be young and an Oriole"—I've said that so many times as a coach and a manager in the minor leagues. It didn't make any difference how old I was, I always put that behind me. I stayed young for a good while, physically and mentally. Being around the game of baseball helps you stay that way.

Chemistry is great, but chemistry doesn't get any hits or get anybody out. If your players don't perform and you don't win, where's your chemistry? You don't have any. If you perform and you win, you have chemistry.

I remember getting off a flight in Miami once, and the Yankees were there as well. Their players weren't really dressed very well, but the Orioles were all in coats and ties. And I said, "I'm proud to be an Oriole. We really look like a major-league club."

My point is that pride does enter into it. There's a multitude of things that enter into it. If you do all the little things, you'll never have one big thing to worry about. In the game of baseball there's nine million little things to do.

Really, that's life. If you do the little things in life, you won't have a big thing to worry about, because you've got your priorities in the right order. You do things in the right order, you help your neighbor, your neighbor helps you, and that's what life's all about, it's the little things. Baseball and life, it's the same.

"It's great to be young and an Oriole"—I've said that so many times as a coach and a manager in the minor leagues. It didn't make any difference how old I was.

AN INTERLEAGUE IDEA

I don't like interleague play. If you want to do something as far as setting up more geographic rivalries, then you've got to redesign everything, and have every region playing in its own league, or its own division, or whatever you want to call it.

In 1961, Jim McLaughlin was farm director for the Orioles. At the time he was studying things as far as economics, which the clubs always did. That year the American League was adding two new clubs, in Los Angeles and Washington, D.C., and the National League was going to add two new clubs the next year, in Houston and New York. Each league was going from eight to ten teams, and they were talking about adding two more teams apiece a few years after that, for a total of twenty-four. Along with expansion, you were talking about increased expenses in terms of travel for every club across the board.

In '61 I wrote a memo for Jim McLaughlin, saying that baseball would have to go to three leagues, or three divisions, in order to operate more cost-effectively. You had two leagues of eight as it was. With expansion, rather than having two leagues of twelve teams, a National League and an American League, it was my idea to go to three leagues of eight. Take the midwestern clubs and put them together, take the eastern clubs and put them together, and take the western clubs and put them together.

Today, considering the cost of going from east to west, that setup would make some sense, but it would have to be a total redesign.

I still say if you want geographic matchups, then redesign the whole thing. Interleague play isn't the way to go. Teams are often playing two-game series, and two-game sets are terrible, particularly with the travel you have to do. You get in at three or four o'clock in the morning, you play that night, and the next day you're packing and going on the road again. Years ago, when clubs weren't traveling to the extent that they are now, they got in to the next city at a reasonable hour.

If you want geographic matchups, then redesign the whole thing. Interleague play isn't the way to go. I'd put all the clubs in the East together, put everybody in the Midwest together, and put everyone in the far West together, and eliminate all that travel.

Unlike a lot of people, I'm not against interleague play from the standpoint of being a traditionalist, although that does bother me to a degree. Changes have to be made, adjustments have to be made, I understand that. You adjust, then you readjust. If it's for the good of everyone concerned, then I think it has to be done. But I don't think that's the case here.

THE
DESIGNATED HITTER
DEBATE

I'd also like to see the designated hitter used through-out the major leagues. That's an adjustment that was made in the game in the American League and through-out the minor leagues. In fact, I was managing the Orioles' Triple A club in Rochester in 1969 the first year that the DH was tried. I had a kid by the name of Jim Campbell who had played first base for me at Double A in Elmira, New York, in '68, and the DH rule allowed him to move up to Rochester the next year and play Triple A ball. He had hit twenty-five home runs at Double A, and the DH rule gave him an opportunity to move up.

The pitchers can't bunt anymore, either, so why not have an offensive player in that spot? Fans want to see offense, and teams have the opportunity there to increase scoring. People talk about how the DH takes the strategy out of the game, but that's not so. The man-ager still has to make up his mind about whether or not that pitcher can still get somebody out when he sends him back to the mound. It's not a case of simply pinch-hitting for the pitcher and bringing in a new pitcher. Many times that's an easier decision to make than to decide whether the pitcher who's out on the mound still has good enough stuff to continue.

The pitchers can't bunt anymore, so let's have an offensive player bat in that spot. Fans want to see offense, and teams have got the opportunity there to increase scoring.

CHAPTER 6

FAMILY TIES

My Most Important Message for Parents

You have to pat your kids on the back, and if they want to play sports—or do anything in life—you should encourage them, not discourage them. Never mind all the chewing out because of a bad play or an error.

A BASEBALL FAMILY

I was on the road quite a bit years ago when I was playing, managing, and coaching, so there were times when
I couldn't be there for the kids, but we made it work. I
used to conduct a lot of clinics when I was managing in
Rochester, and Cal attended those clinics. He once said
that the real reason he went to the clinics was to spend
more time with me. When he'd go to the ballpark when
he was young—he and Billy would take batting practice
prior to the start of my club's workout—he was gaining
more time with me.

Ours was a real baseball family. In Asheville,
North Carolina, when I was managing in the Double A
Southern League, Vi was the chauffeur for the boys, and
she would sometimes go to a Little League game first
and get to our park in the seventh or eighth inning.

In '72, when I was managing at Asheville, thirteen-
year-old Elly was the base sweeper once school was
out, and I believe she operated the scoreboard, too.
Twelve-year-old Cal and seven-year-old Bill were bat
boys, and ten-year-old Fred was the visiting clubhouse
guy. They were all involved with the Asheville Orioles. It

gave all the kids something to do. They were going to be at the park anyhow, so, it was nice.

> *Cal once said that the real reason he went to my baseball clinics was to spend more time with me.*

TWO HEADS
FOR THE GAME

Cal and Billy were fortunate in that they were around the game and had the opportunity to see clubs in the minor leagues, and to see how things were in baseball. They weren't being deceived in any way: They knew before they went into the game that it was a very, very tough business. Our traveling around the country was also a very good education for the entire family.

Cal would come to the ballpark and pay attention to the game. He might come into the clubhouse after the game and say, "Why did so-and-so do this?" And I would explain it to him.

Cal and Billy were always very much interested in playing baseball. When I was managing in the minor leagues, Cal would come to the ballpark and pay attention to the game. He might come into the clubhouse after the game and say, "Why did so-and-so do this?" or, "Why did so-and-so make that play that way?" and I would explain it to him. He would talk to the players, too, and ask them questions about techniques and strategy. Both Cal and Billy gained knowledge from being around the game.

BILLY THE KID

A player like Bill can help a ball club tremendously because he can make a lot of plays at second base. He can turn a double play better than just about anyone, and a double play is a very important part of the game. When he was with the Orioles, I saw him turn a lot of double plays that other second basemen would never have been able to turn. Many times with runners on first and third and one out, we walked off the field without a run scoring. That's an important part of the game, and he was very adept at turning double plays—fielding a tough ground ball, the pivot, the throw—and making plays in general. That type of player is a valuable player for your ball club, but he's undervalued in today's game.

So many times over the course of the season you end up in a first-and-third, one-out situation. If there's a ground ball hit and the double play isn't turned, then that runner at third base scores. If you turn the double play, that run doesn't score.

Bill executed that one-out ground ball for a double play as well as anybody I can ever recall in the game. In fact, I remember a 1987 spring training game in which Durwood Merrill was umpiring at first base. It was that same situation, first and third and one out, and there was a ground ball hit to Cal at shortstop. Bill turned the double play so quickly, and the guy was out at first base by so much, that Durwood missed the play completely.

I went out to argue, and I said, "Durwood, you fouled the play up completely. You had no idea—you anticipated that it wasn't going to be a double play." He said, "I never anticipated that he could make the play that quickly. I've never seen anybody turn a double play that fast." He was anticipating that the runner at first would be safe because of where the ball had been hit. But Cal fielded the ball, got it to Bill at second base, and Bill got rid of it so quickly that it wasn't even a questionable call at first base. The man was out by a step and a half.

That's the type of player you need on a ball club. The Orioles had a tremendous double play combination with Cal at shortstop and Bill at second base. After they got rid of Bill in '93, they had an awful lot of trouble finding a second baseman.

Bill's the type of player you need on a ball club.

In today's game everybody wants home run hitters, and that's fine. Offense is obviously important. But that player in the middle of the diamond also needs to supply defense as well as offense. I've said before that there's no reason that you can't have a big guy playing shortstop, second base, or centerfield. But you don't just want an offensive force at those positions, you want a player who's solid defensively as well.

While Bill isn't going to hit thirty or forty home runs, he's a very dependable offensive player. What's often overlooked in Bill's case, and with so many players who are categorized as lesser hitters, is the way they're used and the contributions they make that don't show up in the box score. For example, Bill would frequently be asked to bunt, he would be asked to hit-and-run, and he would be asked to move runners on the bases, which are valuable things. But when you're doing those sort of things, you're not going to hit for a high average. It's just not conducive to that, because in a way you're getting the bat taken out of your hands.

Rich Dauer is another example. Dauer played second base for me in the minor leagues, and he wasn't blessed with great natural ability, but he worked at his job. He turned the double play well, he made the plays defensively, and he did all the little things that really helped the ball club.

I've told this story at my baseball school a number of times: Once when Dauer was the Orioles' second baseman, we were tied 3–3 in a game against Detroit in the ninth inning. John Shelby, our leadoff hitter, started the inning with a double. Dauer was hitting second, and we wanted him to move Shelby to third base. So Dauer hit a ground ball to the right side of the diamond—not a strong ground ball—that the second baseman caught and threw to first base, so Dauer was out.

That put a man on third, and Cal was hitting third in the lineup. He hit a fly ball to leftfield to drive in the winning run. Sacrifice fly, and we win the ball game 4–3. The headline in the next day's paper was something like: CAL JR. DRIVES IN WINNING RUN IN NINTH INNING. Then, of course, later in the story it was mentioned that Shelby had led off with a double. But there was no emphasis put on Dauer's moving Shelby to third base, which set up the sacrifice fly. That's what I mean when I talk about doing the little things. A guy who does things like that can be so valuable to a ball club.

That's also another example of how there's entirely too much emphasis on statistics in today's game, and not enough emphasis on the ability of the particular player. People focus so much on stats, but they don't always tell the whole story. All Dauer got in the box score was 0-for-1, but it was a productive out: He was responsible for moving that runner to third base.

Bill has had to deal with a lot of injuries in his career. In his first five years in the minor leagues he broke a finger on each hand and had knee and shoulder problems. He only played seventy-five games in his first two pro seasons. He's also had back trouble. All that has been tough on him as far as getting jobs, because teams that liked his abilities and the things he could do said, We'll take a lesser guy because Bill seems to be injury-prone.

I think there were times when the thought of quitting might have crossed his mind. I know I've always told him, "Play as long as you can play, that's the best thing to do." He's battled—he's had all sorts of injuries but he's always done whatever he needed to do to get well and then got back to playing again. He's shown exceptional determination to keep coming back.

He's also had pressure on him coming up through the Orioles system, following Cal, but I think Bill handled all that very well. From the start he said, "I'm not Cal, I'm Bill." They're two different people, and he did the right thing by going out and just being Bill.

Through it all, Bill's personality has always been great. He's a leader, there's no question about it. People might say, Here's a guy who's not hitting for a high average. How can you say he's a leader? With his makeup and the way he goes about the game and the plays he makes, he's always been well-respected by the players on his team. And that's one of the prerequisites of being a leader.

Bill's had pressure on him coming up through the Orioles system, following Cal. From the start he said, "I'm not Cal, I'm Bill." They're two different people, and he did the right thing by going out and just being himself.

THE VALUE OF VI

When the kids were little, Vi and I would pack everybody into the family car and we'd leave home to go to spring training. Then when the kids got in school—and particularly when they were active in their different extracurricular activities, such as sports—they stayed at home in Maryland and joined me after school was out. When I was away Vi was their mother, father, guidance counselor, chauffeur, hitting instructor, pitching instructor, and everything else.

She ran the household. She controlled everything. She took care of them. That's why, when Cal made his speech after breaking Lou Gehrig's consecutive games record, he referred to Vi as "the glue" of the family. Neither I nor any of the children would've been as successful in life as we are if Vi hadn't been there holding everything together.

When I was away Vi was the kids'
mother, father, guidance counselor,
chauffeur, hitting instructor, pitching
instructor, and everything else.

OUR GUIDING PRINCIPLE
FOR RAISING CHILDREN

One thing we always stressed with our kids was that you need to get your priorities in the right order. Then you go out and try to do what you want to do. If you want to be a baseball player, then you've got to go out and give it your best shot to do that. If you want to play the piano, that's fine—whatever you want to do. But you have to go out and give it all you've got.

There are too many people in the world who have to work at a job that they don't enjoy, and then it really becomes just a job. But if you enjoy what you're doing, it's not work. All of our kids had their priorities in the right order and they were able to do the things they wanted to do. They've gone out and represented us very well.

You have to give a young person the opportunity to do what he would like to do. We never forced anything on any of the kids. Cal and Billy wanted to play ball. Fred wanted to come home from school and work on his motorcycle. Well, I encouraged him to do that, if that's what he was interested in. That's the way I think all parents should be.

> *There are too many people in the world who have to work at a job that they don't enjoy, and then it really becomes just a job. But if you enjoy what you're doing, it's not work.*

You can help guide someone along in a field, but if a kid doesn't want to play baseball then I don't think it's right to force him to continue to play. If his interest isn't there, he's not going to put forth the effort that's necessary to do well at it. No matter how much he likes it, no matter how skilled he is, he still has got to work to make himself a better person and a better player. I don't believe you should force someone into something they don't want to do.

> *You have to give a young person the opportunity to do what he would like to do. We never forced anything on any of the kids.*

THE PRIDE
OF PARENTHOOD

People say to us that we're fortunate to have two sons playing in the major leagues, but I'm proud of the way all four of our children developed as individuals. It goes back to when they were growing up. The idea was to let them go out in the world and do what they wanted to do.

Fred now lives in Havre de Grace with his wife and two daughters and he works as a motorcycle mechanic in Delaware, just over the Maryland line. He's coaching Little League girls' softball, and he's just gung-ho about it. His interest right now is tremendous as far as helping those kids get an opportunity to play and enjoy the game of softball.

Ellen also enjoys sports—she just retired from softball a couple of years ago and she enjoyed playing. She and her husband are accomplished bowlers, and they live in Bel Air, and she works for a general contracting company in Towson.

They all enjoy what they're doing. That's 90 percent

of the battle. The family is still very close, so it's nice having everyone in the area for holiday get-togethers. We usually get the whole crew together for Christmas, and sometimes Thanksgiving as well.

I'm proud of the way all four of our children developed as individuals. They all enjoy what they're doing. That's 90 percent of the battle.

SO YOU THINK
YOU'VE GOT A FUTURE
MAJOR LEAGUER?

When you're in professional baseball, whether you're managing, coaching, or scouting, you really don't look at an eight-year-old kid, or a ten-year-old kid, or a freshman in high school, or even a junior in high school as a prospect for professional ball.

Cal did very well in Little League, but I'm not smart enough to know whether a kid who's 8 or 10 years old is going to be a major-league ballplayer. I don't think anybody's that smart. What you do is, when that player becomes a senior in high school, look at the tools that individual has. What kind of arm does he have? What kind of strength does he have? What kind of speed does he have? What kind of bat does he have? What kind of power does he have? What kind of hands does he have? When you look at those things and you say, "These are pretty good tools," then you can say, "This fellow has a chance to be a professional player."

For example, when Cal was a freshman at Aberdeen High School, he was five seven and weighed only 128 pounds. He hit .065 as a freshman. By the time he was a junior in high school, he had gotten much bigger and stronger. He would sometimes come down to the stadium with me and hit and field before our club worked out. When I saw sixteen-year-old Cal hitting the ball into the seats at Memorial Stadium, and I saw him catch ground balls, and I saw the strength of his arm, at that point I said definitely, "Yes, he has a chance to go into professional baseball." But I wanted to look at him the next year when he was a senior to see if he had progressed. Well, of course, I saw that same thing the next year. By then he stood six two and weighed 180 pounds, and he batted .492 as a senior.

> *I'm not smart enough to know whether a young kid is going to be a major-league ballplayer. I don't think anybody's that smart.*

That's the way I've always looked at someone who has the ability to go into professional baseball. I'm usually at the baseball school for registration, and I'm also on the phone a lot with people calling up for applications. I don't know how many times I've heard: "We've got another Cal Jr. on our hands," or "He's going to be the next Rafael Palmeiro." My next question is, "Well, how old is this young man you're talking about?" And they say, "Well, he's gonna be eight," or, "He's gonna be nine," or, "He's ten years old and he's gonna play in the big leagues." Well, I'm not that smart. That's not to take away from the parents' thoughts; they're good thoughts. I just never had those thoughts because of my professional background; because I was involved with the game I just didn't look at my kids that way. When Cal and Billy were that age I just said, We'll wait and see. Let's see how he develops physically, and let's wait until he gets to be fifteen or sixteen and see if the car, or the girls, or something else might influence his thinking.

When I saw sixteen-year-old Cal hitting the ball into the seats at Memorial Stadium, and I saw him catch ground balls, and I saw the strength of his arm, at that point I said definitely, "Yes, he has a chance to go into professional baseball."

THE FOUR D'S

There's definite value for all kids who participate in and play sports. Whether it's baseball, soccer, football, basketball, or another sport, there are great things to be gained.

In the sports world, you learn discipline, and discipline is very important. Also important is the determination to succeed. You need a determination to succeed in sports and you need a determination to succeed in everyday life. You also need the desire to succeed in sports, as well as dedication. In sports you have to be dedicated, you have to be disciplined, and you have to have the desire and determination to do it. You have to display those traits to succeed in every walk of life.

I saw a lot of guys come through the minor leagues who were blessed with all the ability that you'd want to be blessed with, but they lacked the desire to play the game. They lacked the dedication to work at the game. And they didn't make it to the big leagues. I saw some other guys come through the minor leagues who didn't have half the talent that some of these other people had, but they had great work habits, practiced correctly, and worked at their jobs. Eventually, they wound up going to the big leagues.

*In sports you have
to be dedicated,
you have to be
disciplined, and
you have to have
the desire and
determination to
do it. You have to
display those traits
to succeed in every
walk of life.*

COPING WITH CANCER

Every year we have a crab party for the staff over at the baseball school, and we have a big time. Well, we had the party one Saturday last September, as usual, but I was feeling kind of bad that day. I wasn't bouncing around too well, and I was tired, which is unusual for me. Then on Sunday we had Elly's bowling team over for a few crabs. Vi said that she thought I had had a stroke or something, I looked so bad. So the next day we went to the doctor and he put me in the hospital for tests.

The next day they transferred me from Harford Memorial Hospital in Havre de Grace to Johns Hopkins in Baltimore. Then all the fuss began. Naturally, the first thing right out of the cracker barrel was that I had lung cancer and some other spots where there was cancer. I didn't know anything about cancer, I didn't know what any of the options were. It became a matter of the doctor telling me what I had to do. This hit close to home because a few days later, on October 6, Mark Belanger, the outstanding former Orioles shortstop who had played for me for years and who was a great friend, died of lung cancer at age fifty-three.

So I listened to the doctors. Based on their study, and where the cancer is, the type of treatment they recommended was radiation and chemotherapy. Well, I took fourteen treatments of radiation and four rounds of chemo by the end of the year.

Unfortunately, around the third or fourth week after the first chemotherapy treatment, I came down with a serious rash and then a swelling. It was diagnosed as a reaction to one of the medications they were giving me. Well, it was like somebody had poured scalding water over my entire body, inside and outside. They coated me with creams and ointments three times a day.

For days I said, "Well, tomorrow has got to be better than today." But tomorrow got here and it wasn't even as good as the previous day. I continued to do what had been prescribed. When we finally got the rash pretty well curtailed, some other annoying rashes popped up. I couldn't swallow, I felt like I was all burnt inside. I was in the hospital twice during that early period, for five days the first time and fifteen days the second.

For days I said, "Well, tomorrow has got to be better than today." But tomorrow got here and it wasn't even as good as the previous day.

The problem with my reaction was that they couldn't give me anything to counteract it. It just had to run its course. I looked like a burn victim—in fact, they said I had some third-degree burns because of it. Then my skin got brown and it just didn't peel once, because more than one layer of skin had been burnt, it peeled off several times.

Eric Davis of the Orioles was taking chemo and playing ball. Well, he wasn't dealing with what I've been dealing with and playing ball. Of course, he's a lot younger than I am and he didn't have the reactions that I've had. It wasn't until about early December that I was really able to get up and get dressed.

By the time the rashes were cleared up, I had all new skin over my entire body. With the new skin, we had to get some extra heaters for the house because I was so cold. The skin takes a while to toughen up. Early on it was very, very tender, even my hands. I don't like the cold weather, and to me, anything below 80° is cold. Now with all this new skin, anything below about 95° was cold. I knew from the beginning that it was going to be a while before I could get out and about, and that it would require a lot of work inside first. I've got to keep working at it.

In my whole life I had never even been in the hospital before this. I told the doctors, "It took me sixty-two years to get here, and you're doing sixty-two years worth of work on me while I'm here." CAT scans, X rays, MRIs, transfusions, bronchoscopies . . .

There were days when I had some tough things to

do. On some of those days I didn't think I had ever had anything tougher than that to deal with in my life. But they tell me that if I do this, and I do that, they think they're going to be able to curtail this thing. Now all we have to do is try to get this accomplished. The whole thing has obviously been a big adjustment for me, dealing with all these treatments, because I'm used to being out and doing things.

There were days when I had some tough things to do. On some of those days I didn't think I had ever had anything tougher than that to deal with in my life.

THE OUTLOOK

I've had a terrific support network around me, between the family and friends. You won't find any better. That does help. I know I have a close family, but now that I've witnessed it in action, it has made a difference. Also, our friends have been there for me, and even strangers. Many people who I didn't even know have written me notes of encouragement. We've got a big bag full of letters and cards. It's very supportive.

It's a long, hard road, I can tell you that. They don't have to tell me that, either, because I know it is. I know it's going to take a while to get strong again and be able to do things, but I've just got to do it. It's going to take time.

I wasn't what you'd call a negative person before this, but I was one to face the fact that that wasn't a positive over there, that was a negative. I don't care how long you looked at it, it wasn't going to become a positive. So you'd better face the damn fact that that was a negative, and then go from there.

*I wasn't what you'd call a
negative person before this, but I
was one to face the fact that that
wasn't a positive over there, that
was a negative. I don't care how
long you looked at it, it wasn't
going to become a positive. So
you'd better face the damn fact
that that was a negative, and
then go from there.*

I've always been very much a realist, there's no question about that. Hope isn't worth a damn.

My outlook is positive, but I don't think that because I've got a positive attitude, I'm going to get cured. I believe that you've got to be positive and do the things that are going to allow you to get better. I don't have much choice but to do that.

FOR THE RECORD

Calvin (Cal) Edwin Ripken, Sr.

BORN: December 17, 1935

HEIGHT: 5'11" WEIGHT: 170

BATS: Right THROWS: Right POSITION: Catcher

PROFESSIONAL STATS

YEAR	CLUB	LEVEL	GAMES	ABS	RUNS	HITS	DOUBLES	TRIPLES	HRS	RBIS	AVG.
1957	Phoenix, AZ	Class C	112	398	68	109	15	6	7	60	.274
1958	Wilson, NC	Class B	118	393	40	85	20	2	4	38	.216
1959	Pensacola, FL	Class D	61	219	36	64	14	3	2	35	.292
	Amarillo, TX	Double A	30	69	6	14	2	0	0	3	.203
1960	Fox Cities, WI	Class B	107	356	59	100	20	4	9	74	.281
1961	Little Rock, AK	Double A	32	81	6	15	2	1	1	8	.185
	Leesburg, FL	Class D	52	127	20	30	3	0	1	13	.236
	Rochester, NY	Triple A	11	24	2	2	0	0	1	2	.083
1962	Appleton, WI	Class D	58	143	25	39	9	0	4	36	.273
1963	Aberdeen, SD	Class A	—Did not play—								
1964	Aberdeen, SD	Class A	2	1	0	0	0	0	0	0	.000
Totals			**583**	**1,811**	**262**	**458**	**85**	**16**	**29**	**269**	**.253**

Calvin (Cal) Edwin Ripken, Sr.

MANAGERIAL RECORD

YEAR	CLUB	LEVEL	LEAGUE	W–L	PCT.
1961	Leesburg, FL	Class D	Florida State	37–36	.507
1962	Appleton, WI	Class D	Midwest	61–63	.492
1963	Aberdeen, SD	Class C	Northern	65–55	.542
1964	Aberdeen, SD*	Class C	Northern	80–37	.684
1965	Tri-City, WA	Class A	Northwest	81–58	.583
1966	Aberdeen, SD	Class A	Northern	47–22	.681
1967	Miami, FL	Class A	Florida State	65–76	.461
1968	Elmira, NY	Double A	Eastern	77–63	.550
1969	Rochester, NY	Triple A	International	71–69	.507
1970	Rochester, NY	Triple A	International	76–64	.543
1971	Dallas-				
	Ft. Worth, TX	Double A	Texas	82–59	.582
1972	Asheville, NC**	Double A	Southern	81–58	.583
1973	Asheville, NC	Double A	Southern	71–69	.507
1974	Asheville, NC	Double A	Southern	70–67	.511
1975	—Orioles scout—				

(continued)

YEAR	CLUB	LEVEL	LEAGUE	W–L	PCT.
1976–86†	Baltimore	—Orioles coach—			
1985	Baltimore (June 13)	Majors	American	1–0	1.000
1987	Baltimore	Majors	American	67–95	.414
1988	Baltimore	Majors	American	0–6	.000
1989–92		—Orioles coach—			
Totals				**1,032–897**	**.535**

*Won pennant; named Northern League Manager of the Year

**Won pennant

†Orioles won pennants in 1979 and '83 and World Series in '83

Calvin (Cal) Edwin Ripken, Jr.

BORN: August 24, 1960

HEIGHT: 6'4"   WEIGHT: 215

BATS: Right   THROWS: Right   POSITION: Shortstop/Third Base

PROFESSIONAL STATS

YEAR	CLUB	LEVEL	GAMES	ABS	RUNS	HITS	DOUBLES	TRIPLES	HRS	RBIS	AVG.
1978	Bluefield, WVA	Rookie	63	239	27	63	7	1	0	24	.264
1979	Miami, FL	Class A	105	393	51	119	28	1	5	54	.303
	Charlotte, NC	Double A	17	61	6	11	0	1	3	8	.180
1980	Charlotte, NC	Double A	144	522	91	144	28	5	25	78	.276
1981	Rochester	Triple A	114	437	74	126	31	4	23	75	.288
	Baltimore	Majors	23	39	1	5	0	0	0	0	.128
1982	Baltimore	Majors	160	598	90	158	32	5	28	93	.264
1983	Baltimore	Majors	162	663	121	211	47	2	27	102	.318
1984	Baltimore	Majors	162	641	103	195	37	7	27	86	.304
1985	Baltimore	Majors	161	642	116	181	32	5	26	110	.282
1986	Baltimore	Majors	162	627	98	177	35	1	25	81	.282
1987	Baltimore	Majors	162	624	97	157	28	3	27	98	.252

(continued)

YEAR	CLUB	LEVEL	GAMES	ABS	RUNS	HITS	DOUBLES	TRIPLES	HRS	RBIS	AVG.
1988	Baltimore	Majors	161	575	87	152	25	1	23	81	.264
1989	Baltimore	Majors	162	646	80	166	30	0	21	93	.257
1990	Baltimore	Majors	161	600	78	150	28	4	21	84	.250
1991	Baltimore	Majors	162	650	99	210	46	5	34	114	.323
1992	Baltimore	Majors	162	637	73	160	29	1	14	72	.251
1993	Baltimore	Majors	162	641	87	165	26	3	24	90	.257
1994	Baltimore	Majors	112	444	71	140	19	3	13	75	.315
1995	Baltimore	Majors	144	550	71	144	33	2	17	88	.262
1996	Baltimore	Majors	163	640	94	178	40	1	26	102	.278
1997	Baltimore	Majors	162	615	79	166	30	0	17	84	.270
1998	Baltimore	Majors	161	601	65	163	27	1	14	61	.271
Minor league totals			**443**	**1,652**	**249**	**463**	**94**	**12**	**56**	**239**	**.280**
Major league totals			**2,704**	**10,433**	**1,510**	**2,878**	**544**	**44**	**384**	**1,514**	**.276**

William (Billy) Oliver Ripken Jr.

BORN: December 16, 1964

HEIGHT: 6'1"   Weight: 190

BATS: Right   THROWS: Right   POSITION: Second Base/Shortstop/Third Base

PROFESSIONAL STATS

YEAR	CLUB	LEVEL	GAMES	ABS	RUNS	HITS	DOUBLES	TRIPLES	HRs	RBIS	AVG.
1984	Hagerstown, MD	Class A	115	409	48	94	15	3	2	40	.230
1985	Charlotte, NC	Double A	18	51	2	7	1	0	0	3	.137
	Daytona Beach, FL	Class A	67	222	23	51	11	0	0	18	.230
	Hagerstown, MD	Class A	14	47	9	12	0	1	0	0	.255
1986	Charlotte, NC	Double A	141	530	58	142	20	3	5	62	.268
1987	Rochester	Triple A	74	238	32	68	15	0	0	11	.286
	Baltimore	Majors	58	234	27	72	9	0	2	20	.308
1988	Baltimore	Majors	150	512	52	106	18	1	2	34	.207
1989	Baltimore	Majors	115	318	31	76	11	2	2	26	.239
1990	Baltimore	Majors	129	406	48	118	28	1	3	38	.291
1991	Hagerstown, MD	Double A	1	5	1	3	0	0	0	0	.600
	Frederick, MD	Class A	1	4	2	1	0	0	0	1	.250

(continued)

YEAR	CLUB	LEVEL	GAMES	ABS	RUNS	HITS	DOUBLES	TRIPLES	HRS	RBIS	AVG.
	Baltimore	Majors	104	287	24	62	11	1	0	14	.216
1992	Baltimore	Majors	111	330	35	76	15	0	4	36	.230
1993	Texas	Majors	50	132	12	25	4	0	0	11	.189
1994	Texas	Majors	32	81	9	25	5	0	0	6	.309
1995	Buffalo	Triple A	130	448	51	131	34	1	4	56	.292
	Cleveland	Majors	8	17	4	7	0	0	2	3	.412
1996	Baltimore	Majors	57	135	19	31	8	0	2	12	.230
1997	Texas	Majors	71	203	18	56	9	1	3	24	.276
1998	Toledo	Triple A	5	19	3	6	1	0	0	1	.316
	Detroit	Majors	27	74	8	20	3	0	0	5	.270
Minor league totals			**566**	**1,973**	**229**	**515**	**97**	**8**	**11**	**192**	**.261**
Major league totals			**912**	**2,729**	**287**	**674**	**121**	**6**	**20**	**229**	**.247**

ACKNOWLEDGMENTS

Many thanks to Pocket Books senior editor Jane Cavolina, a first-rate pro who believed in this project from the start and whose insights and patience were invaluable commodities. This book also may never have left the batter's box were it not for the vision and savvy of Scott Waxman, who helped pull the whole concept together. The considerable efforts and talents of *Sports Illustrated* writer–reporter Lars Anderson are, as always, greatly appreciated. Ira Rainess and Désirée Pilachowski of the Tufton Group provided much crucial behind-the-scenes assistance. Marlene MacLeod and Lynn Remy were always more than willing to go the extra mile on the transcription front, for which they deserve a great deal of thanks. The copyediting work of fellow Regian Rob Stauffer helped immensely. Thanks also to fellow Lous Lee Harrs, Pete Labbat, and Greg Giraldo for their support. And the Ripken family, especially Cal, Sr.; Vi; and Cal, Jr., are as good as advertised: always professional, and often inspirational.

—L.B.

ABOUT THE AUTHORS

Cal Ripken, Sr., has spent most of his life playing or coaching the game of baseball, including thirty-eight years in the professional ranks with the Baltimore Orioles. A former professional catcher (he also played some third base and outfield and even pitched in the pros), he played six-plus seasons in the minor leagues for the Orioles. He went on to manage in Baltimore's farm system for thirteen-plus seasons (1961–74), the longest tenure of any minor-league manager in Orioles history. Since retiring as a player after the 1962 season (he was a player-manager in 1961 and '62) he had only one losing season as a minor-league skipper. He won the first of his two pennants and was named Northern League Manager of the Year in 1964 after leading his Class A Aberdeen, South Dakota, club to an 80-37 record. He finished first again in 1972 with Asheville, North Carolina, of the Double A Southern League.

During the 1975 season he worked as a scout for the Orioles, primarily at the professional level. He joined the Baltimore coaching staff in 1976, serving mainly as third base coach during his tenure there. He was named

Orioles manager before the 1987 season and held that job until early 1988, when he was fired six games into the season. In 1987, as manager of Cal, Jr. and Bill, he became the first father ever to manage two sons simultaneously in the major leagues. He returned as a Baltimore scout in June of 1988, and came back as third base coach in 1989. He left the Orioles after the 1992 season, and was inducted into the club's hall of fame in 1996.

Cal, Sr. has managed at five different professional levels and owns a combined 1,032-897 (.535) record as a manager in the majors and minors. He has also served as a coach for two American League pennant winners (1979, '83) and one World Series winner (1983).

He works closely with and makes regular appearances at the Cal Ripken Baseball School, which enters its fifteenth year of operation in 1999. The school is for players ages eight to eighteen and is conducted during the summers (late June–early July) on the campus of Mount Saint Mary's College in Emmitsburg, Maryland.

The sixty-three-year-old Cal, Sr. lives in Aberdeen, Maryland, with Vi (Violet), his wife of forty-one years. Vi was honored in 1988 as Maryland's First Lady of Baseball. The Ripkens have four children: Ellen Leigh; Cal, Jr.; Fred; and Bill.

A lifelong baseball enthusiast, **Larry Burke** is a senior editor for *Sports Illustrated,* the author of *The Baseball Chronicles: A Decade-by-Decade History of the All-American Pastime* and the co-author (with Johnny

Bench) of *The Complete Idiot's Guide to Baseball*. Formerly the editor of *Inside Sports* magazine, he has worked as a sportswriter for the *South Bend* (Indiana) *Tribune* and has covered major-league baseball for the Associated Press, United Press International and several major newspapers. A native of Nutley, New Jersey, and a graduate of the University of Notre Dame, he lives in Darien, Connecticut, with his wife, Beth; sons Casey and Charlie; and daughter, Maddie. In Darien he has served as a Little League umpire and as a member of the town's Little League Board of Directors.